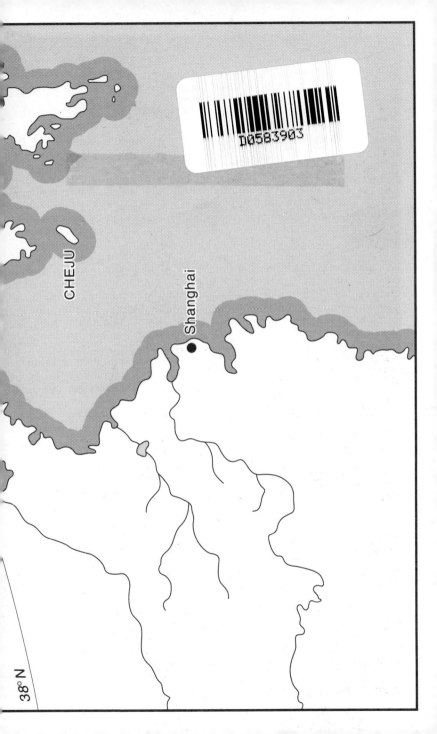

Korean Musical Instruments

Series Editors, China Titles:
NIGEL CAMERON, SYLVIA FRASER-LU

Korean Musical Instruments

KEITH HOWARD

HONG KONG
OXFORD UNIVERSITY PRESS
OXFORD   NEW YORK
1995

Press

k
k Bombay
Salaam Delhi
bul Karachi
id Melbourne
Singapore
Taipei Tokyo Toronto

and associated companies in
Berlin Ibadan

Oxford is a trade mark of Oxford University Press

First published 1995
This impression (lowest digit)
1 3 5 7 9 10 8 6 4 2

Published in the United States
by Oxford University Press, New York

© Oxford University Press 1995

British Library Cataloguing in Publication Data
available

Library of Congress Cataloging-in-Publication Data

Howard, Keith, 1956–
Korean musical instruments / Keith Howard
p.   cm. — (Images of Asia)
Includes bibliographical references, discography, and index.
ISBN 0-19-586177-9
1. Musical instruments — Korea I. Title.   II. Series.
ML537.H68   1995
784.19519—dc20   95-31765
CIP
MN

Printed in Hong Kong
Published by Oxford University Press (China) Ltd
18/F Warwick House, Taikoo Place, 979 King's Road,
Quarry Bay, Hong Kong

Contents

Preface

KOREA is all too frequently dismissed as merely a cultural outpost of its two mighty neighbours, China and Japan. Nonetheless, although cultural assimilation has occurred, Korea has a long-standing, distinct, and independent culture worthy of our attention. For many of us, it remains veiled and distant; publications about the peninsula have not yet made inroads into our knowledge and understanding. The few early writers on Korea focused their interest on the 'exotic', travel writers still rarely visit, and many of the academic dissertations published about the culture remain relatively inaccessible to those unable to experience the country firsthand. The knowledge many have of Korea starts at the end of the Second World War, when a partition of the peninsula was imposed. Over time, this division led to the development of a socialist North and a capitalist South. The partition, and its results, has given ammunition to political scientists and economic analysts but has tended to shift attention to theory and away from life and culture—the unique sights and sounds of Korea's countryside and cities.

Here I try to share something of the culture's uniqueness, as well as to reflect regional differences and commonality. I try to integrate—for the first time—the musical instruments of both parts of the Korean peninsula. My approach seems appropriate, particularly since Koreans on both sides of the divide long for unification. I divide instruments into strings, woodwinds, and percussion, using terminology based on the system devised by Hornbostel and Sachs.[1] Classification numbers are given in brackets, following the shorthand 'H/S'. This system has little place in Korean tradition; it is now, however, preferred by a number of scholars since local classifications tend to reflect court usage at the expense of the folk heritage, or merely list instruments from the most common to the rare and obsolete. My romanizations of Korean terms follow the McCune–Reischauer system, as adopted in 1984 by the Ministry of Education in Seoul.[2] The occasional Chinese terms are given in *pinyin* romanization. Pitch is marked from the piano's middle C, here c´, with octaves as c´´, c´´´ ascending, and c, C, C´ descending.

The translation of indigenous terms is always contentious. I have tried wherever possible to keep the Korean names of instruments, since I feel that simple glosses, which too often substitute the names of similar Western instruments, introduce an unacceptable Eurocentric bias. Similarly, I feel that historical sources, and the names of musical genres, are usually better left in Korean. My aim throughout has been clarity. This has led me, for instance, to gloss the two surviving sacrificial rites, *Chongmyo cheryak* and *Munmyo cheryak*, as 'Rite to Royal Ancestors' and 'Rite to Confucius' since, despite the Sino-Korean characters, nothing happens in either that matches the definition of 'sacrifice' given in the *Oxford English Dictionary*.

Since 1981, I have conducted my research in the countryside, in Seoul, and in P'yŏngyang. I am indebted to many instrument makers, teachers, performers, and students, particularly those at the Korean Traditional Performing Arts Centre (*Kungnip kugagwŏn*) in Seoul, Seoul National University, P'yŏngyang Music and Dance College, the Isang Yun Music Research Institute (*Yun Isang ŭmak yŏn'guso*), and the People's Instrument Improvement Collective (*Minjok akki kaeryang saŏpkwa*). I am responsible for all the photographs except for the pictures of Pak Kyunsŏk and Yi Pongju, which are reproduced courtesy of the Office for Cultural Assets, Seoul. The notation for *haegŭm* was written by Kim Kisu and published in *Haegŭm chŏngak* (Seoul: Kungnip kugak kodŭng hakkyo, 1979). Tuning systems for North Korean instruments are abstracted from Pak Hyŏngsŏp's *Tanso* (P'yŏngyang: Munye ch'ulp'ansa, 1983) and Han Namyong's *Haegŭm* (P'yŏngyang: Munye ch'ulp'ansa, 1983). Other line drawings first appeared in my *Korean Musical Instruments: A Practical Guide* (Seoul: Se-kwang, 1988).

This small volume can do little more than merely scratch the surface of a fascinating music culture. It is an introduction, and a general survey, of instruments in use now or preserved from the recent past on the Korean peninsula. I hope it will stimulate interest, an interest that is long overdue.

[1] E. M. von Hornbostel and Curt Sachs, 1914. An English translation by Anthony Baines and Klaus P. Wachsmann is published as 'Classification of Musical Instruments', in *Galpin Society Journal* 14: 3–29 (1961). I have also made use of Nazir Ali Jairazbhoy's more recent article, 'An Explication of the Sachs-Hornbostel Instrument Classification System', in *Selected Reports in Ethnomusicology, Volume VIII: Issues in Organology*: 81–104 (Los Angeles: University of California, 1990).

[2] Anon, 'The romanization of Korean according to the McCune-Reischauer system', in *Transactions of the Korea Branch of the Royal Asiatic Society*, 38: 121–8 (1961). The Ministry of Education allows for '*shi*' rather than '*si*', a convention I adopt here (for example, using 'Shilla' and not 'Silla' and '*shijo*' not '*sijo*'), since this gives a better indication of sound.

1

The Cultural Context for Korean Music

THE KOREAN PENINSULA juts out from the mainland of East Asia between the latitudes 43° and 33° north and longitudes 124° and 134° east. One thousand kilometres connect its southernmost island with the mountains and rivers that mark the northern land borders with China and Russia. Korea has a temperate climate, with temperatures ranging from a frigid -15°C during the far north's winter to a high of 35°C in summer in the central provinces. The coastline is rugged, snaking for 17,361 kilometres and encompassing 3,500 islands to give a total landmass of 221,000 square kilometres, roughly the same size as mainland Britain. Mountains cover 70 per cent of the territory and are celebrated in paintings and poetry, yet they impede agriculture. They feature in geomancy, along with rivers almost equally prized and feared since they are prone to devastating floods. Forty-four million people live in South Korea and about 23 million in North Korea. If the current desire for unification is achieved, Korea will rank as the world's fourteenth largest nation in population.

Korea's remoteness is legendary: it was known as the Hermit Kingdom during its last dynasty, Chosŏn (1392–1910). Yet, it has long had considerable strategic importance, since it straddles the major trade route from China to Japan. The Koreans claim a 5,000-year history; many would add that this mirrors their long history as an independent state. They claim descent from Tan'gun, the mythical son of a bear born on Paektu Mountain in the north, and hold tenaciously to their homogeneous identity, despite numerous invasions, such as those by the Mongols in 1231 and 1254, the Japanese in 1592–8, and the Manchus in 1627 and 1636.

They proudly contest that they invented movable type in 1234 (200 years before the Germans) and iron-clad ships in the 1590s (centuries before the Americans). Korea, then, is neither a Chinese cultural appendage nor a Japanese economic satellite.

To maintain their cultural integrity, Koreans have had to balance the demands of powerful neighbours. For many centuries, a regular tribute system ensured relatively peaceful relations with China. The court emphasized a Chinese-style examination system and developed a civil service modelled on that of China and maintained by a top-down class system based on Chinese Confucianism. Japanese culture was kept at a suitable distance. Occasional envoys were dispatched to Japan, and trade was channelled solely through an isolated trading house in the south-eastern port of Pusan via the Japanese island of Tsushima. Other foreigners were distrusted, and few set foot on the peninsula until international treaties were signed in the late nineteenth century. For a brief time, despite a primitive monetary system and little to trade, Korea emerged suddenly but tentatively from its self-imposed isolation. It was subsumed, however, into the Japanese empire after the Sino-Japanese and Russo-Japanese wars of 1894–5 and 1904–5. The Hermit Kingdom was sealed once more when Japan took control of foreign relations and then formally made Korea a colony in 1910.

In 1945, after the abrupt end of the War in the Pacific, the suffering of Koreans hardly ceased. Two junior Washington officers proposed a temporary partition along the 38th parallel, so that the Soviets and Americans could divide responsibility for taking the Japanese surrender. The partition created a division roughly equal in terms of territory and left the capital, Seoul, advantageously in the southern half. Two rival governments soon emerged. In the south, the American military command quickly let their intolerance towards communist sympathizers be known. They chose the stability of the old and failed to oust those who had collaborated with the Japanese. As a consequence, the 1948 elections supervised by the United Nations south of the parallel allowed the ageing Syngman Rhee (1875–1965) to be declared president of the Republic of Korea. Rhee's family was related to royalty, and he consolidated his power mainly through the landed gentry. North of the parallel, Soviet sponsorship allowed the emergence of the Democratic People's Republic of Korea, led by Kim Il Sung (born Kim Sŏngju, 1912–94). Kim had been a minor guerrilla fighter against the colonial power (although the current hagiography has it that he was the paramount guerrilla leader). Under Kim's totalitarian regime it was inexpedient to be a landlord, a collaborator with the Japanese, or a Christian.

Korea arrived squarely on the world stage as a result of interstate rivalry. A civil war erupted on 25 June 1950. With a United Nations pledge of support for the southern forces, the conflict soon became an international one. The Korean peninsula was where the Cold War turned hot: an East Asian crisis tested European, American, and Asian concerns about communist expansion. The resulting tragedy left three million Koreans dead and much of the culture's tangible heritage destroyed.

Contemporary Western images of Korea often reflect the conflict and immediate postwar development. This is unfair, for North and South each emerged as a phoenix from the ashes of destruction. The bustle of the two capitals, P'yŏngyang in the north and Seoul in the south, belie the Japanese-inspired appellation, 'Land of Morning Calm'. The lingering picture of poverty also no longer reflects the reality: in the late 1950s per capita GNP in the South stood below US$100, lower than that of India, but by 1994 it had reached US$8,400, snapping at the heels of several European Community states. The fifteenth-largest global economy and the eleventh-largest trading nation, the South is now known for its industry and hard-working populace. The North began even more dramatically, and postwar reconstruction greatly improved people's lives. It remains a bastion of socialism, trumpeting *juche [chuch'e]*, a unique but ultimately chimerical philosophy of self-reliance. But the North's economy, built around outdated heavy industry and the support of compliant citizens, has since the mid-1970s fallen rapidly behind that of the South.

Approaches to music and musical instruments differ in the two states. The South inherited the mantle of cultural nationalism, a dogma developed in the 1920s by the founders of Korean folklore studies to counter Japanese attempts at assimilation. The primary watchword has been that the old must be maintained. After National Assembly debates in the 1950s, the year 1962 saw the promulgation of the *Munhwajae pohobŏp* (Cultural asset preservation act) by the incoming military regime of Park Chung Hee. The new law aimed to rebuild national pride. Nationhood, it asserted, had been devastated by the colonial period, by war, and by subsequent reliance on American aid. The law set up a mechanism to appoint *poyuja* (holders) of *muhyŏng munhwajae* (intangible cultural assets). A group of scholars was charged with the recovery and restoration of 'authentic' forms of performance arts and crafts. The government encouraged regular events such as the *Chŏn'guk minsok yesul kyŏngyŏn* (National folk arts contest) and other exhibitions. By the end of 1992, 94 cultural assets had been appointed (numbered from 1 to 99, allowing for deletions). These comprise 17 musical genres, 7 dances, 14 dramas, 22 plays and rituals, 31 manufactures, and 3 additional assets concerned with food preparation and martial arts.

Government sponsorship generally concentrates on what is threatened or dying; it supports genres that belong to outmoded lifestyles or which in everyday life have been superseded by crafts and arts largely imported from Europe, America, and Japan. Some observers have maintained that the asset system thereby creates 'synthetic' forms, but many South Koreans would disagree, arguing that the system has promoted a uniquely Korean identity. During the 1970s and 1980s nationalism was on the rise, as increasing urban affluence created space for nostalgia. A revival began in the musical sphere, and tradition (*chŏnt'ong*) now prospers. The focus on regional, rural, indigenous, and largely oral folk arts has remained that of cultural nationalism. Performance of traditional arts, however, has shifted from the country-side to urban stages: who wants to sing planting and weed-ing songs in the fields when tractors have replaced manual labour? And support now comes in differing political colours. State sponsorship at venues such as the *Kungnip kŭkch'ang* (National theatre) and *Sŏul Nori Madang* (Seoul outdoor performance space) must now contend with an equally pernicious presence, namely the *madanggŭk* (outdoor theatre) performances prominent in anti-govern-ment student demonstrations.

The maintenance of high culture, much of which was imported from China for exclusive use in the court, has been achieved by retaining and encouraging old organiza-tions. In 1907, 305 musicians were employed at the court music institute; only 30 remained in 1945. Fewer still, 17, refounded the institute in the Pusan enclave during the Korean war. Today, the same institute, now renamed the Korean Traditional Performing Arts Centre (*Kungnip kugag-wŏn*), employs over 200 musicians, dancers, and researchers. Since the institute preserves old music and rites, it is the major client of craftsmen sponsored within the asset system to preserve the art of instrument-making. The institute has also been aided by South Korean musicologists. The senior scholar, Lee Hye-Ku (b.1909) helped to develop a post-colonial discipline for the study of Korean music that was firmly anchored in history and literature. Until the late 1980s, Korean musicology was primarily concerned with the discovery, interpretation, and comparison of written scores and sources, a focus which sidelined much of the oral folk tradition.

After the war, cultural activity in the North began by adapting socialist realism. Andrei Zhdanov, in the Soviet Union, had defined this style in 1932 as both historic and dynamic: 'Art must depict reality in its revolutionary development'. Kim Il Sung used Mao Zedong's *Talks on Literature and the Arts at Yan'an* as a filter for his own version: artists were to be engineers of the human soul, their works learning from the lofty spirit of ordinary people and serving the people as powerful weapons. It was inevitable that cultural policy would reflect political more than aesthetic concerns. In the 1950s, as the nation was reconstructed along socialist lines, revolutionary songs and the marches of military bands were promoted. Programmatic music, modelled on that heard in Moscow and on the earlier expressionist style fostered by composers such as Kim Sunnam and Yi Kŏnu, was matched to titles that kept the ancient Chinese custom of telling the audience exactly what the music was about. Examples would include Kim Sunnam's *Kŏn'guk haengjin'gok* (Foundation march for the nation), Yi Kŏnu's *Kanŭn kil* (The way to go), and Kim Wŏn'gyun's *Hyangt'o* (My country).

The beginnings of a shift came in 1957, with the *Ch'ŏllima undong* (Galloping horse movement). Socialism had been established, collective ownership enforced, and independence from Soviet and Chinese models was now fostered. Kim Il Sung felt secure: he rationed art, standardized themes and materials, and looked to the people for inspiration. This was not simply a foreshadowing of China's Cultural Revolution, for North Korean musicologists were sent to the countryside to collect and notate vernacular folk-songs. These they arranged to be suitable for the Revolution, homogenized in a style based loosely on that of the north-western region but with new texts, less ornamentation, and with diatonic rather than the old pentatonic melodies. The *Ch'ŏllima undong* allowed the reintroduction of some indigenous instruments, particularly those which could be allied to the folk tradition.

The 1970s saw *juche* grow as a national policy of self-reliance. Two further control strategies were imposed at this time on artistic production, *chŏngjaron* (seed theory) and *chipch'e ch'angjak* (collective creation). The former emphasized content over form, while the latter exercised control over individualism. *Juche* focused on domestic consumption, remodelling and upgrading the indigenous by incorporating foreign elements. Symphonic music staged a comeback, and an updated opera, centred on the *P'i pada kagŭk tan* (Sea of blood opera company), evolved by echoing Chinese examples. It is in this context that the activities of the *Minjok akki kaeryang saŏpkwa* (People's instrument improvement collective) became important. Old instruments (*ko akki*) were to be 'improved' (*kaeryang*) to increase their flexibility. They were to keep Korean timbres, but they must combine these with all the techniques available to their Western orchestral counterparts. The 'improvements' were made to court popularity; old instruments were to be enabled to compete with Western counterparts, particularly those instruments beloved in *kyŏng ŭmak* (light music) bands.

The demands of socialist reconstruction and the head-long rush to modernize has meant that in both Koreas the dominant musical culture is of Western origin. Western music was first experienced in Korea about a century ago as the hymns of missionaries and the bands of European and American armies. This new music soon overcame traditional styles at both missionary and colonial state schools. The pervasive influence continues today. In South Korea, a Top-40 pop chart of *Han'guk kayo* (Korean songs) is published every week. Each song is modelled on Western pop equivalents, from ballads and 'unplugged' to reggae and rap. In 1990, there were 428 documented traditional music concerts, attracting less than 8 per cent of the total nation-wide audience, compared to 2,719 concerts of Western music. At the same time, the classical radio station, KBS-FM 1, devoted more than 78 per cent of its air time to Western music and only 14 per cent to Korean music. Korean music accounted for around 16 per cent of recorded music sales. These figures include three song genres—patriotic *kagok*, children's *tonggyo*, and popular *yuhaeng-ga*—developed earlier in the century with harmony, melody, and instrumentation modelled on Western styles. In these genres, only the texts are Korean. Such song genres, sometimes arranged and reinterpreted as purely instrumental *ppongtchak* (an onomatopoeic term for the typical fox-trot rhythm), still provide the musical wallpaper of South Korea's coffee-shops and restaurants. They also form the backbone of North Korea's popular music.

Where appeals to the formation of tradition once precluded any notion of the composer, the influence of Western individualism has led to a vibrant composition scene, one still largely modelled on that found in the West, as is witnessed in the studies and works of the 1,539 Bachelor's degree-level composition majors registered at 13 South

Korean universities in 1989. Perhaps the best-known Korean composer is Isang Yun (b.1917), resident in Berlin but with a reputation that reaches across Europe. Yun was born in the south, however he is now a regular visitor to North Korea, where an institute, the *Yun Isang ŭmak yŏn'guso*, experiments with advanced Western-style composition. Nonetheless, ideology demands that P'yŏngyang composers write popular music (*taejung ŭmak*), hence it is only south of the border that the avant-garde can be seen to flourish. Also, only in South Korea has a significant movement developed to compose *shin kugak*, new music for traditional instruments. Some composers, such as Kim Kisu (1917–86), trained at the court institute; others, such as Hwang Byung-ki (Hwang Pyŏnggi, b.1936), are expert performers on traditional instruments. Many, however, initially study Western-style composition and feel the need to push the boundaries of the old as they create novel ensembles to capture harmonic depth and explore timbral contrasts.

Western culture may remain ascendent, but in both North and South Korea respect for indigenous music is slowly increasing. Nationalism contrasts the hedonism and rationalism of the West with emotional ties to the indigenous. Ask Koreans what they appreciate in Western music and they will likely describe form, structure, and order. But, ask what appeals in Korean music and typical responses will focus on feelings. Western music can only be taught; Korean music tugs at the heartstrings. Korean music—and, by extension, Korean musical instruments (Plate 1)—alone reflect the air, the water, and the soil of the Korean peninsula.

2

The Musical Tradition

THE SILK ROAD, a system of trading routes that stretched more than 11,000 kilometres across the heart of Asia, brought together merchants from China and the regions of Central Asia, and reached onto the Korean peninsula as well. In the early centuries of the first millennium AD, music with roots in the Near East and India merged with Central Asian and native Chinese styles before passing to Lolang, a military outpost of the Chinese empire. Lolang, near modern P'yŏngyang, survived from 108 BC to AD 313 and initiated the first sustained contact between Han Chinese and the culture of the peninsula. Some of the earliest references to Korean music thus occur in Chinese sources. Chen Suo's third-century *Sanguo zhi* describes how people in Mahan, to the south-west of Lolang, sang and danced at times of planting and harvesting.

Tomb paintings of the time also illustrate musical scenes that indicate Chinese interaction with the peoples of the area. Wall murals in the third Anak tomb, completed about AD 357 to house the remains of a Chinese official, portray Chinese instruments in a Korean setting. In the front-room mural a singer is accompanied by panpipes (*xiao*) and standing drum (*gu*). In the main corridor a procession is followed by a band of drum, panpipes, horn (*qiao*), and handbell (*nao*). And in the rear room another singer is accompanied by seated musicians playing the zither (*zheng*), lute (*yuanxian*), and flute. Across the Chinese border, in Manchuria's Jilin province, murals in the fifth-century Changchuan Tomb No. 1 depict nine instruments, some similar to Chinese models but, reflecting their assimilation, all can be given Korean names: a transverse flute (*hoengjŏk*), a vertical flute (*changso*), two lutes (*ohyŏn pip'a* and *wan-ham*), a zither (*kŏmun'go*), a five-string zither (*ohyŏn'gŭm*), a long horn (*taegak*), an oboe (*p'iri*), and a suspended drum (*tamgo*).

Korea has a literary tradition stretching back at least to the eighth century AD, but many important manuscripts have been lost during the invasions of the last thousand years. To reconstruct musical history, we must rely on ret-rospective indigenous accounts, which impose political and philosophical notions relevant to the time they were writ-ten, and on more contemporaneous Chinese and Japanese writings. The *Samguk sagi* (History of the Three Kingdoms), written in 1145 by Kim Pushik (1075–1151), is the most significant surviving indigenous source for information con-cerning the period up to the tenth century. The less rig-orous *Samguk yusa* (Romance of the Three Kingdoms), by the monk Iryŏn (1206–89), provides some additional infor-mation. Thus, we know that among the three kingdoms dominant in the first centuries AD, Koguryŏ (in the north and west; traditional dates 37 BC–AD 668) sent ensembles to the Chinese Sui court. The people of Koguryŏ favoured the Central Asian lute (in Chinese, *yuanxian*; in Korean, *pip'a*) and cylindrical oboe (*p'iri*). It was in Koguryŏ that the *kŏmun'go* zither was invented. Paekche (in the south-west and centre; 18 BC–AD 660) imported the harp (in Chinese, *gonghou*; in Korean, *konghu*) and a flute with a raised mouthpiece (*chi*) from south China. Paekche developed rela-tions with Japan, and in the seventh century one of its musicians, Mimashi, taught mask dances learnt in China at the Japanese court.

Samguk sagi provides a legend that describes how the *kayagŭm* zither was created on the orders of Kaya's King Kashil. Kaya, a tribal federation situated along the south coast of the peninsula, was absorbed by Shilla (initially in the south-east; 57 BC–AD 668) in the sixth century. There, the *kayagŭm*, along with the transverse flute, became an important court instrument. The following Unified Shilla dynasty (668–935) controlled most of the peninsula and developed a characteristic 'three strings, three winds' (*samhyŏn samjuk)* ensemble. The ensemble boasted the Shilla *kayagŭm*, Koguryŏ *kŏmun'go*, Central Asian *pip'a*, three sizes of transverse flutes—big (*taegŭm*), medium (*chunggŭm*), and small (*sogŭm*)—and clappers (in Chinese, *paiban*; in Korean, *pak*) from Tang China. The term *hyang-ak* began to be used at this time to differentiate local genres from those of the Chinese. Buddhist chants, now known as *Pŏmp'ae* and preserved in South Korea within Asset No. 50, *Yŏngsanjae* (Plate 2), were imported from China. A memorial to the master Chin'gam credits him with its introduction to Korea: he went as an emissary to the Tang court in 804 and only returned in 830.

Officially dated 1451, Chŏng Inji's *Koryŏsa* (History of the Koryŏ dynasty) describes the music of the next dynasty, Koryŏ (918–1392). This text, like the *Samguk sagi*, is a ret-rospective evaluation and divides Koryŏ court music into three types: *aak* (Chinese ritual music played in what was considered an authentic style), *tangak* (other music of Song Chinese origin), and *sogak* (indigenous music). In the world of music, the most significant events of the dynasty occurred in the years 1114 and 1116, when the court received two gifts from the eighth emperor of the Chinese Song court, Huizong. Threatened by Khitan and Jurchen attacks, Huizong believed it worthwhile to strengthen ties with Korea. The gifts, often considered by historians to be an ill-contrived political bribe, were actually requested by the Koreans. The state religion of Koryŏ had officially been Buddhism, but national political philosophy was increasingly articulated in terms of Confucianism. Korean kings had begun to observe Confucian rites to heaven (*Wŏn'gu*), agriculture (*Chŏkchŏn*), land and grain (*Sajik*), and royal ancestors, and they needed suitable music for the rites. The first gift, of *dasheng xinyue*, music for banquets, was of limited use, although consisting of an impressive 167 instruments, scores, and illustrated instructions for performance. The second gift, in 1116, was more desired by the Koreans: it was *dasheng yayue*, music for rituals. It comprised a massive 428 instruments together with costumes and ritual dance objects, but since the Chinese emperor required greater respect than did a suzerain state, the total forces were less than they would have been in China. *Dasheng yayue* became Korea's *aak*. The instruments were divided into a terrace ensemble (*tŭngga*) and a courtyard ensemble *(hŏn'ga)*. The first performance took place in October 1116 before King Yejong (r.1105–22) at the Kŏndŏkchŏn Royal Audience Hall. The size of these two gifts and their specific uses begins to explain why many instruments in Korea have limited provenance.

Koryŏsa established the Confucian mould which was to mark subsequent theses and manuscripts on music. It ostensibly ignored folk music, although by 1188 indigenous Korean music had been added to some of the rites. This was consistent with earlier practice, for Koryŏ had begun with three state rites, all of which are thought to have shared common secular songs, dances, and acrobatics. *P'algwanhoe* had been an ancient prayer for national peace addressed to mountain and river spirits; elements of it are considered to survive in mask plays such as that preserved at Hahoe village in North Kyŏngsang province. *Yŏndŭnghoe* looked to the Buddha for blessings, and *Narye* had been an annual court exorcism.

Virtually all of the Chinese instruments at court were lost in the 1361 invasion. Moreover, as Confucianism took hold in the following dynasty, Chosŏn, boundaries between folk and court became less permeable. In 1430, the need to keep appropriate rituals, the loss of instruments, and the infiltration of indigenous music combined to lead four government officials—Yu Sanul, Chŏng Inji, Pak Yŏn, and Chŏng Yang—to revise the ritual music. The revision is documented in the *Aakpo* (Notations of ritual music), appended as two chapters to the *Sejong shillok* (Annals of King Sejong; compiled 1452–4). In this work, 456 potential melodies and transcriptions are prescribed, of which today only six are played in a single rite, the biennial *Munmyo cheryeak* (Rite to Confucius)(Plate 3). The six comprise five transpositions of one basic melody (with *fa* as C, E, F, G#, and A, respectively) followed by a second melody in the final section of the rite. Each is played in a uniform way, with eight equal phrases of four regular notes. Formulaic percussive patterns mark the ends of phrases and the beginning and end of each melody. In what appears to be a uniquely Korean development, each tone is played with a slow ascending glissando.

A second extant court rite, the annual *Chongmyo cheryeak* (Rite to royal ancestors), uses two song suites, *Pot'aep'yŏng* (Preserving the peace) and *Chŏngdaeyŏp* (Founding the dynasty), which were composed during the reign of King Sejong (r.1418–50) and are recorded in the *Sejo shillok* (Annals of King Sejo; compiled 1469–71). The remaining Chinese music, the *tangak* repertory, was soon Koreanized, and today only two pieces are still played, now only in orchestral versions: *Nagyangch'un* (Spring in Lolang) and *Pohŏja* (Walking in the void).

Korean composition took a large step forward in 1446 following the promulgation of the Korean alphabet, *han'gŭl*. A long poem celebrating the alphabet, *Yongbi ŏch'ŏn'ga* (Dragons fly up to heaven), was set to two melodies. These are no longer sung, but an expanded orchestral version, *Yŏmillak* (The king shares pleasure with his people), based on a Chinese translation of the text and set to a modified Chinese-style hexatonic melody, does survive.

The fifteenth century ended with the publication of Sŏng Hyŏn's musical compendium *Akhak kwebŏm* (Guide to the study of music; 1493)(Fig. 2.1). Predating any compa-

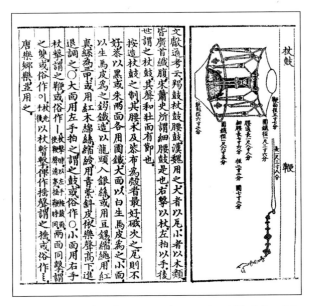

2.1   The entry for *changgo* in the treatise *Akhak kwebŏm*.

rable treatise in Europe, *Akhak kwebŏm* quotes Chinese sources and gives notations and prescriptions for rituals and dance. The text divides music into ritual *aak* (with 37 instruments listed as *abu akki*), Chinese *tangak* (with 13 *tangbu akki*), and indigenous *hyangak* (with 7 *hyangbu akki*). *Akhak kwebŏm* omits a few instruments, such as the *tanso* flute, and as an indication of Confucian respect

15

for the suzerain Chinese the still-popular *kayagŭm* zither is relegated to the native category. The division mixes the then-contemporary function of each instrument with its supposed origin.

A different classificatory system used elsewhere subjugates these concerns beneath a consideration of materials. This is the Chinese-originating *p'al ŭm* ('eight sounds') system, which divides instruments into those made of bamboo, wood, metal, silk, skin, stone, gourd, and clay. Here, too, something of the origins can still be relevant. For example, the *saenghwang* (mouth-organ) is classified as a gourd. This reflects the windchest of many centuries ago, but the gourd has long been superseded by metal, wood, or lacquer. Mythical associations also mean that the *saenghwang* is distinguished in the *p'al ŭm* system from the clay *hun* (ocarina) and the bamboo *so* (panpipes). Precision, however, is compromised in that the sound-producing material is not clearly differentiated from the body material. Thus, the *yanggŭm* (dulcimer) is categorized as silk although it has metal strings, while the *t'aep'yŏngso* ('great peace pipe') and *p'iri* are classified as wood and bamboo, respectively, although they share double-reed agitators.

Local classifications of instruments are more varied and stand in marked contrast to such systems. Most ignore ritual instruments and account only for those instruments found in the countryside. The ubiquitous percussion drums and gongs, which provide the quintessential rhythmic underpinning for songs and generate the atmosphere for dance and entertainment, are typically described in terms of the brash and hard verb *ch'ida* (to hit). In contrast, melodic instruments are considered to require more skill and, since they imitate the voice or attract spirits in shamanistic rituals, they are typically talked about in terms of relaxed and smooth verbs such as *nolda* (to play) and *hada* (to do).

16

In Chosŏn society, the literati monopolized education to control access to the *mun'gwa* and *chapkwa* civil service examinations. Beyond the confines of the court, however, a new musical culture developed. Normally associated with the emergence of a group of professionals, the *chungin*, during the late seventeenth century, this music came to be known as *chŏngak* ('correct music'). The *kŏmun'go* zither was central within it, providing the lead for ensembles known as *p'ungnyu* or *chul p'ungnyu*. The most sophisticated surviving *chŏngak* chamber piece is the suite *Yŏngsan hoesang* (the name derives from syllables matched to the opening notes in the oldest surviving score: 'Buddha preaching on Spirit Mountain'). New styles of vocal music also emerged, including *kagok* (lyric songs)(Plate 4), *kasa* (narrative songs), and, later, *shijo* (sung short poems).

The literati left many manuscripts, the majority of which provide notations for the *kŏmun'go* in a mixture of *hapchabo* tablature, onomatopoeic *yakpo*, and the basic pentatonic palette of *oŭm yakpo*. Examples include the *Kŭm hapchabo* (An Sang's zither score; 1572), *Yanggŭm shinbo* (Yang's new zither score; 1610), and *Yuyeji* (Chapter on artistic amusement; late eighteenth century). A more precise 12-tone notation system, *yulchabo* (after the Chinese *lulu*) was at this time confined to ritual music, for which it was used in the annals of Sejong and Sejo. It began to be more widely used in and after the late nineteenth century *Sogak wŏnbo* (Original source of popular music). In South Korea, with the addition of comprehensive ornament symbols, most of which were devised by the composer and musicologist Kim Kisu, *yulchabo* is now the standard pitch notation in instrument workbooks.

The court retained musicians from the Unified Shilla period onwards. Documentation is patchy, however, and at different periods recruitment methods and the terms of

17

employment varied. At times musicians were seconded from government or army ranks; intermittently, they were imported from the countryside, and often they were born into families of musicians. Heredity, and movement between the court and the country, indicates a longstanding amateur/professional interface. Such an interface becomes important in any consideration of Korean folk music, for the distinction concerns status. Although musical skill was prized by the aristocracy, and playing or listening to music remained an acceptable pastime for the literati, court documents regularly reported the supposed depravity of professional musicians. The latter were not allowed to own land and were grouped within the virtually outcast *ch'ŏnmin*, along with shamans, monks, butchers, pallbearers, and handicraftsmen. Professional musicians seem to have developed from a number of preceding groups. The *hwarang* 'flower boys' of Shilla, among the earliest of these, was formed to promote artistic, ethical, and military training by King Chinhŭng (r.540–76). They performed alongside female counterparts, the *kisaeng* (entertainment girls), at court entertainments such as the *P'algwanhoe*. Declaring their activities irreligious, King Sŏngjong (r.982–97) finally expelled them. New troupes evolved as *sadang*, *namsadang*, and *kŏsa*; they were often based near mountain temples, particularly after King T'aejong (r.1401–18) banished the children of concubines from the court.

During the Chosŏn period, male musicians were known as *kwangdae* and *chaein*. Relations between male musicians and female shamans (Korean shamans are predominantly female) have been close (Plate 5). Indeed, musicians at shamanistic rituals are still called *hwarang* in remote parts of South Korea, and it would seem that the husbands of shamans have often been musicians in their own right.

In the realm of professional folk music, *p'ansori* (epic

storytelling for solo singer accompanied by *puk* drum) and *sanjo* ('scattered melodies' for solo instrument and *changgo* drum accompaniment) remain particularly popular. *P'ansori* (Fig. 2.2) is a composite art form developed by

2.2 A performance of *p'ansori*, Korea's solo operatic form, with An Suksŏn accompanied on the *puk* by Chŏng Hwayŏng. An, from Namwŏn, was a student of the renowned Kim Sohŭi (1917–94) and is probably the most popular singer in Korea today.

kwangdae musicians that combines song (*sori*), narration and dialogue (*aniri*), and simple dramatic action (*pallim*). Each *madang* (story) is long and can take five or more hours to perform in its entirety; traditionally, it was normally given in instalments. The singer wears a Korean costume, *hanbok*, and may hold two props—a fan in the right hand and a handkerchief in the left. The drummer, known as the *kosu*, has a vital role: not only does he keep a constant and repeating rhythmic cycle (*changdan*), but he adds shouts of encouragement known as *ch'uimsae*. His importance is suggested by the expression *il kosu i myŏngch'ang* (one drummer is worth two singers). Although the genre is often assumed to stretch back into the distant past, the earliest documentary source for *p'ansori* is a 1754 text by Yu Chinhan. 'Eight great singers' are known from the late eighteenth century and twelve *madang* are listed in Sŏng Manjae's (1788–1851) poem *Kwanuhŭi*. *P'ansori* singers were male until the impresario and civil servant Shin Chaehyo (1812–84), a collector and arranger of *p'ansori* texts, introduced the first female singer. By then, *p'ansori* was popular among the middle and upper classes and had absorbed literary allusions and Confucian moralism. Five *madang* survive: *Ch'unhyangga* (The song of 'Spring Fragrance'), *Shimch'ŏngga* (The song of Shim Ch'ŏng), *Hŭngboga* (The two brothers), *Sugungga* (The underwater palace), and *Chŏkpyŏkka* (The red cliff). In South Korea a few new adaptations have appeared, including Pak Tongjin's *Yesujŏn* (The story of Jesus) and Im Chint'aek's setting of the poet Kim Chiha's *Ojŏk* (Five enemies).

Ch'anggŭk, an adaptation of *p'ansori* to an operatic staged format that was perhaps influenced by Peking Opera, premiered in 1903 in Seoul at Korea's first national theatre, the Hŭidae. *Ch'anggŭk* survives in the South, where it has been criticized for subsuming creative art beneath theatrical effect. *Ch'anggŭk* and *p'ansori* have been rejected in the North: not only were they part of the colonial legacy, but Kim Il Sung objected to the élitist, non-revolutionary nature and raspy vocal character of the underlying model, commenting, 'It is ridiculous to imagine soldiers rushing to battle inspired by *p'ansori*.' It could be surmised that *ch'anggŭk* sought to counter the inroads made by Western music, but the first performance by Koreans of a European opera, Giuseppe Verdi's *La Traviata*, was mounted in Seoul only in 1948. Opera had little place in pre-1945 Korea, thus the claims of North Korean composers—led by Kim Wŏn'gyun (b.1917)—that *P'i pada kagŭk tan* introduced a new opera style suitable for Korea and Koreans may not be unreasonable. In North Korea, *P'i pada* (The sea of blood) premiered in 1971, and it was quickly followed by *Kkŏt panŭn ch'ŏnyŏ* (The flower girl), *Ch'unhyangjŏn* (The Story of 'Spring Fragrance'), *Tang ŭi ch'amdwin ttal* (A true daughter of the party), *Kŭmgangsan ŭi sori* (Song of Mount Kŭmgang), *Yŏnp'ungho* (Gentle breeze), and *Millima iyagi hara* (Tell the story, Forest). All conform to the same *P'i pada* style. They are said to be 'immortal', since they relate the exploits of revolutionary heroes. Structurally, they replicate folk-song melodies, use a mixed orchestra of Western and Korean instruments, abandon coloratura arioso in favour of more simple strophic songs, and add an off-stage chorus known as *pangch'ang* that interprets the action.

During the same period, in South Korea the loss of traditional entertainment venues left *p'ansori* facing near terminal decline. In the 1960s, the genre became Asset No. 5, but, faced with a disinterested public, few performers could eke out a living. Only in the 1970s, after a *p'ansori hakhoe* club had been founded, were regular performances mounted in Seoul. Audiences grew and recordings began to be released. *P'ansori* entered a new era, and its popularity was cemented with the extraordinarily successful 1993 release of a film produced by Im Kwŏnt'aek, *Sŏp'yŏnje*. The film told the story of a wandering singer and his daughter. *P'ansori*, in the tradition, was sung in one of two styles: *Sŏp'yŏnje*, 'Western style', uses lyrical and emotional singing in contrast to the more common, brash, and masculine 'Eastern' *Tongp'yŏnje*.

Sanjo is considered to have developed from *p'ansori*, folk songs, and the shaman music of Korea's south-western Chŏlla provinces. Many claim Kim Ch'angjo (1865–1920) invented the genre. As an amateur rather than a professional musician close to the literati, Kim probably initiated the performance of a solo piece devoid of ritual associations. *Sanjo* was first played on the *kayagŭm* zither, but it was adapted in 1896 by Paek Nakchun (1876–1930) for the *kŏmun'go* zither. Pak Chonggi, Chi Yonggu, and Ch'oe Ŭngnae soon developed versions for the *taegŭm*, *haegŭm*, and *p'iri*. Today, there are a number of schools attributed to master players for each instrument. The schools for *kayagŭm sanjo* stand as memorials to celebrated musicians who have all since died: Kim Chukp'a (real name Kim Nanch'o; the granddaughter of Kim Ch'angjo), Kang T'aehong, Kim Yundŏk (Kim's school is preserved by the *kayagŭm sanjo* asset-holder Yi Yŏnghŭi), Pak Sanggŭn, Ch'oe Oksan (preserved until her death in 1994 by the asset-holder Ham Tongjŏngwŏl), and Sŏng Kŭmyŏn.

Sanjo was once taught entirely by rote but, as training moved to university music departments in the 1960s, scores began to appear. *Sanjo* is now the most popular folk instrumental genre in the South, and a single performance can last around an hour. In the North, it is still taught but rarely performed. It has been updated: Chŏng Namhŭi, the former teacher of Kim Yundŏk, played a shortened 10–15 minute version on the 21-string 'improved' *kayagŭm* until his death in the mid-1980s. And in P'yŏngyang, flute performers describe their *sanjo* as '*hyŏndae*' (contemporary). In effect, *sanjo* has been replaced by new pieces considered to match more closely the ideal of populist *minjok ŭmak* (people's music) promoted since the *Ch'ŏllima undong* movement began. Some pieces, such as the zither trio *Pada ŭi norae* (Song of the sea) and the fiddle solo *Amudo mulla* (Nobody knows), are based on revolutionary songs. Others are modelled after folk-songs, including *Yŏnggang kinari* for shawm and drum, *Onghiya* for *kayagŭm* ensemble, and *Hwanggŭmsan ŭi paek toraji* (The white bell-flower of

Yellow Gold Mountain) for the recently developed harp zither *ongnyugŭm*. A few, like *Pom* (Spring), written in concerto-style but also learnt as a solo study, retain the once-favoured programmatic approach.

In rural Korea, egalitarianism and communal activities have ensured an abundance of group genres. Folk-songs (*minyo*) have been common to accompany work, for entertainment, and for commemorations of death. Folk bands (now known by the umbrella term *nongak*)(Plate 6) were until recently used in village rites (for example, *maegut*), for fund-raising (*kŏllip, kŏlgung*), farming (*p'ungmul*) and fishing (*ture*), and entertainment (*p'an'gut*) activities. The amateur/professional interface was equally evident in this aspect. We can thus make a distinction between *t'osok minyo* and *t'ongsok minyo*. The term *t'osok* refers to local customs, and includes songs that fit standard European definitions of folk music, in that they are functional, have no composers, and have unknown, oral histories. Styles are distinguished that are roughly congruent to dialect areas. *Namdo minyo*, from the Chŏlla provinces, are based on a sorrowful tritonic *kyemyŏnjo* mode. Vocal sadness, known as *aewan ch'ŏng*, couples to considerable chest resonance and a tight throat. *Kyŏnggi minyo*, from the central region around the southern capital, Seoul, are joyful and lyrical. *Sŏdo minyo* were once featured in P'yŏngan and Hwanghae provinces in the north-east. The most characteristic old folksong, *Sushimga*, is preserved by migrants around Seoul as part of Asset No. 29; in the North, the characteristic full and wide vibrato and gushes of emotion have been ironed out in favour of lyrical diatonicism.

North Korea has, in essence, taken up the mantle of *t'ongsok minyo*, popular songs with wider provenance. Such songs are often called *shin minyo* (new folksongs) or add '*t'aryŏng*' to their title. These were the songs of the professionals, recorded since the 1920s by *p'ansori* experts and urban singers on the Japanese-owned Victor and King labels. Still today, most commercial folk-song recordings in South Korea, and virtually all published folksongs in North Korea, are of, or derive from, the *t'ongsok* repertory.

A similar division exists in contemporary folk bands. The three regional styles—*udo* around the rice plain of Chŏlla, *chwado* in the more hilly areas further east, and *kyŏnggi* in the central Kyŏnggi and Ch'ungch'ŏng provinces—survive in festivals but are increasingly rare in the countryside. The year 1978, however, saw a new urban phenomenon: *SamulNori*, a four-man band playing updated pieces from each region on the four basic percussion instruments, two gongs and two drums. *SamulNori* sit where local *nongak* bands stood, marched, and danced. *SamulNori* play a repertory that develops sequences of rhythmic patterns in fixed time-frames, while local bands improvised around simple rhythmic models. And *SamulNori* have proved remarkably popular. They have spawned several dozen professional rivals; urban performances range from student groups to a massed band of 1,100 that played at the opening ceremony for the 1993 Taejŏn Expo. The latter, in the words of one drummer, was indeed a 'Big Bang *SamulNori*'.

1. Postage stamps, issued in Seoul, depicting musical instruments.

2. Buddhist monks perform on wooden slit drums and gongs in the ritual *Yŏngsanjae*, from South Kyŏngsang province.

3. The Rite to Confucius, presented by a courtyard orchestra and dancers, showing the director, *p'yŏn'gyŏng* stone chimes, and *pyŏnjong* bronze bells.

4. Kagok lyric song, performed by a male singer accompanied by the *Chŏngnong akhoe* ensemble.

5. A shaman addresses house spirits in a ritual from Chindo, South Chŏlla province. The shaman plays a *ching*, while the musicians play the *p'iri*, *changgo*, *puk*, and *ajaeng*.

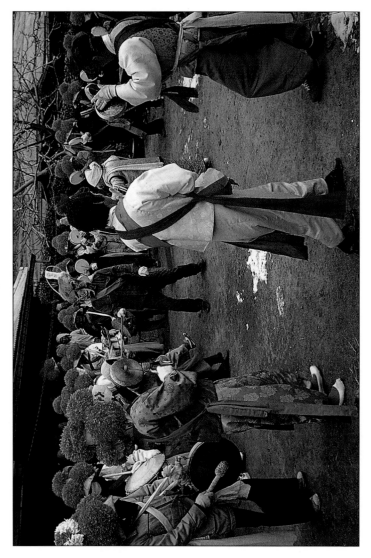

6. A *nongak* percussion band from Sangman village, Chindo, performing at New Year.

7. *Picnic by the Lotus Pond,* by Shin Yunbok (1758–?), showing the court *kayagŭm.*

8. Yi Yŏngsu, holder of Asset No. 42, string instrument manufacture, making *kayagŭm* bridges in his workshop.

9. Detail from a pottery jar from the fifth–sixth century AD, showing an early *kayagŭm*.

10. Girls learning the 'improved' *kayagŭm* at the Man'gyŏngdae Children's Palace, P'yŏngyang.

11. The *kŏmun'go*.

12. The *haegŭm* in South Korea.

13. The 'improved' *haegŭm* in North Korea.

14. The *ongnyugŭm*.

15. The *taegŭm*.

16. The traditional *tanso*.

17. The *p'iri*, showing the embouchure and oversize bamboo reed.

18. Kang Hansu (1928–88), a celebrated shaman musician, plays a plastic *p'iri* with one hand and simultaneously adds a second instrument in a ritual.

19. Kim Pyŏngsŏp (1921–87) demonstrating his *changgo* dance.

20. The *t'aep'yŏngso* accompanying a percussion band.

21. A local Chindo musician dancing with the *puk* (note the use of two sticks).

22. Pak Kyunsŏk (1919–86), the late holder of Asset No. 63, *puk* manufacture, stretches the skin over a wooden body.

23. Yi Pongju, holder of Asset No. 77, brassware manufacture, casting a gong.

24. The *kkwaenggwari* player in a professional *SamulNori* group.

3

String Instruments

In the 1960s, the journalist Ye Yonghae wrote an article decrying the imminent loss of ancient crafts, such as the making of string instruments:

Traditional Korean instruments incorporate the ancient philosophy of 'heaven and earth, male and female, four seasons, five lines'. Master artisans must be in the stage of nothingness, completely integrated with nature. It is said that the instrument maker's search after the perfect sound can be likened to a saint's search after perfect righteousness.

The old craft has not died. In South Korea, Kim Kwangju (1906–84) was appointed holder of Asset No. 42, *akki ch'ang* (string instrument manufacture) in 1971. And, in North Korea, instruments have been brought into the industrial age through the manufacture of 'improved' versions.

Kim Kwangju was known for his *kayagŭm* and *kŏmun'-go*. The *kayagŭm*, the most popular South Korean instrument, is a 12-string half-tube plucked zither (H/S 312.22.5)(Plate 7). It resembles the Chinese *zheng*, Mongolian *yatga*, Japanese *koto*, and Vietnamese *dan tranh*. All these instruments descend from a common model, the ancient *zheng*. Some have 12 and some 13 strings, and a Chinese story tells why: two *zheng* resulted when quarrelsome siblings split a 25-string *se* into two instruments. The term *kayagŭm* translates as 'zither from Kaya', a reference to an invention legend and also the reason why Koreans consider this a purely indigenous instrument.

Two distinct traditional versions of the *kayagŭm* survive. The larger, known as the *pŏpkŭm, p'ungnyu kayagŭm*, or *chŏngak kayagŭm* (*pŏp* = law; *p'ungnyu* = elegant music; *chŏngak* = 'correct music'), is associated with court and literati ensembles. This version has a body made from a single piece of paulownia wood (*odong namu*). Old wood from high rocky areas such as the Sŏrak, Chiri, or Songni mountains is preferred, cut at a slight angle from the core of the trunk to generate the appropriate round and slightly damped sound. The front of the body is planed and burnished to give a convex surface, and a soundbox is hollowed out through a large rectangular rear hole. Twelve silk strings, wound and immersed in boiling water to give strength, are attached to pegs (*tolgwae*) above a fixed hardwood bridge (*hyŏnch'im*) near the top of the instrument. The strings pass over movable bridges known as *anjok* or *kirŏgi pal*, 'wild geese feet', because of their two-toed shape (Plate 8). The bridges have a slightly bulbuous, indented top, rather like bishops or pawns in European chess. They are made from jujube or cherry and are bought in sets connected by a thread ending in a decorative tassel. The strings are wound in coils behind cord loops at the lower end of the soundboard. In turn, the cords (*pudŭl*) are threaded around and through an extension to the body: the characteristic sandalwood *yangidu* 'ram's horns'. From the very earliest examples, the ram's horns have set the *kayagŭm* apart from all other East Asian zithers. Curiously, the cords are never knotted, since the ram's horns provide sufficient friction to hold the strings tense.

The second traditional version of the *kayagŭm* is today known as the *sanjo kayagŭm*. It has a body similar to that of the *chŏngak kayagŭm*, with a convex front board of paulownia but sides and back of a hard wood such as chestnut. The backpiece usually has three soundholes fashioned as a new moon (*ch'osaeng tal*) above a stylized character for happiness (*hŭi*) and the full moon (*porŭm tal*). Many older instruments have carved inscriptions. The smaller size facilitates the rapid flurries required in *sanjo* as the performer's hand flits between strings. Perhaps because this instrument was used by travelling musicians, the design reduces the prominence of the ram's horns to make the instrument more portable.

Three extant pottery artefacts show a similar instrument with distinct ram's horns, dating the *kayagŭm* to the fourth century AD or earlier (Plate 9). One, a tall jar known as the *changgyŏngho*, was excavated at the Shilla capital, Kyŏngju, in 1974. Dated tentatively to the reign of Mich'u (r.262–84), the jar shows a pregnant woman who plays the zither beside a snake. A steamer lid tells a similar story, but the player appears alongside a sexually aroused dancing man. Could the *kayagŭm* have been used in some sort of fertility cult? The invention legend in *Samguk sagi* indicates a later date for the instrument's development. It describes how King Kashil, ruler of the Kaya tribal federation, heard a *zheng* and commented that since countries do not share languages they should not have the same music. U Rŭk, a musician from Sŏngyŏl prefecture, was ordered to compose music for a new instrument. He did so, giving names based on places in Kaya to 12 pieces: *Hagarado, Sanggarado, Pogi, Talgi, Samul, Mulhye, Hagimul, Sajagi, Kŏyŏl, Sap'alhye, Isa,* and *Sanggimul*. The titles suggest the appropriation of local folksongs. Around 551, U Rŭk fled to Shilla, where King Chinhŭng allowed him to settle in Kugwŏn (in today's North Ch'ungch'ŏng province). A year later, Pŏpchi, Kyego, and Mandŏk were sent by the king to learn U Rŭk's music. The three considered it unrefined and reworked it as five new pieces suitable for the Shilla court: the new instrument had become respectable. Four eighth-century *kayagŭm,* catalogued as *Shiragi koto* ('zithers from Shilla'), survive in the Shōsōin repository at Nara, Japan.

In the fifteenth century, *Akhak kwebŏm* associated the *kayagŭm* with indigenous musical forms. Thereafter, it led a liminal existence on the edge of ensembles at the Confucian court. The *kayagŭm* is played seated on the ground with the top of the instrument resting on the right knee, the body falling away to the left. The soft fleshy part of the right hand fingers pluck the strings and ornaments are added by the left hand fingers beyond the bridges. Its attraction in contemporary Korea reflects its versatility. As a solo instrument, it is the most common one used for *sanjo* pieces and is favoured by composers. It has a wide range, with a lower register welcomed by ensembles and a high register capable of accompanying the voice.

New versions of the *kayagŭm* have appeared in the twentieth century, largely as a consequence of its use. The first seems to have been the short-lived *kahyŏn'gŭm*, an attempt to amalgamate the *kayagŭm* with the six-string zither, *kŏmun'go*. The *kahyŏn'gŭm* simplified the tuning process by replacing cords with pins and mounted the instrument on a stand. In North Korea, the 'improved' *kayagŭm* learnt much from this version (Plate 10). Metal wrest pins and hitch pins now tune and hold 21 nylon strings. The increased number of strings allows missing diatonic pitches to be accommodated, introducing the potential for harmonic and heterophonic structures unknown in Korea's monophonic tradition. The use of nylon strings increases volume but decreases noise elements and the slow attack envelopes of the old *kayagŭm*, thereby encouraging virtuosity at the expense of serenity.

The 1980s saw parallel developments in South Korea. In 1982, the instrument maker Yi Yŏngsu (b.1929)—now a holder of Asset No. 42—was asked to devise a 12-string instrument suitable for use in the ensemble accompanying *ch'anggŭk*. His response was to increase the potential volume by enlarging the old *kayagŭm*. In 1984, the composer and theorist Yi Sŏngch'ŏn (b.1936) commissioned Kim Kwangju's successor, Ko Hŭnggon (b.1951), to make two new instruments. One was to be a scaled-down version of the *sanjo kayagŭm* designed as a first instrument for small children. The second was designed to increase the range and volume of the old instruments, and in February 1985 Ko showed this new 21-string version. Three strings were pitched below those of the old 12-string *sanjo kayagŭm* and six above, to give a total range of four octaves. The traditional construction remained, however, a significant drawback since low and high pitches lacked resonance. Nonetheless, the new instrument could better match Western solo instruments such as the piano, as was demonstrated in Yi Sŏngch'ŏn's most celebrated piece to date, *Pada* (The sea), premiered in 1986. The two instruments were soon absorbed as soprano and bass in a novel ensemble together with the *sanjo kayagŭm* (Fig. 3.1).

3.1 Close-up of a 1992 record sleeve, showing a trio of three different *kayagŭm* in South Korea.

In 1990, the performer Hwang Pyŏngju devised a further instrument that is fast becoming standard issue in Seoul-based orchestras. Said to be modelled on modern *zheng*, this version has nylon strings and wrest pins and hitch pins common to the northern instrument although, given political exigencies, the similarities are not admitted. The 17 strings give a three-octave range. Hwang overcomes the problem of resonance by varying string thickness, from 2.15mm on string 1 to 0.8mm on string 17, and restores the paulownia backpiece of court instruments. He has aimed to accommodate the needs of all traditional repertories. Hence, his instrument overlaps the low scale of the court (E^b–a^b) with a typical *sanjo* range (F–c˝), and adds higher tones to better match female singing (up to f˝).

The second zither, *kŏmun'go* (Plate 11), has an even more impressive history than does the *kayagŭm*. Literati often call it the *hyŏn'gŭm*, a name derived from the Sino-Korean *hyŏnhakkŭm* (black crane zither). *Samguk sagi* cites a legend which tells how a Chinese *qin* was kept in the Koguryŏ court. Nobody knew how to play it, so the king offered a reward that persuaded Wang Sanak to remodel it as the *kŏmun'go*. As Wang played his new instrument a black crane flew into the room and danced (hence the alternative name, although the presence of a crane echoes common Chinese stories where they symbolize longevity). Scholars favour a date around the end of the fourth century for the invention, but there is little firm evidence. When Shilla unified the peninsula, the *kŏmun'go* became a part of court ensembles. In Chosŏn times, reflecting its prominent entry in *Akhak kwebŏm* (Fig. 3.2), it was the primary literati instrument. A nineteenth-century poem about Seoul, *Hanyangga*, contains the lines:

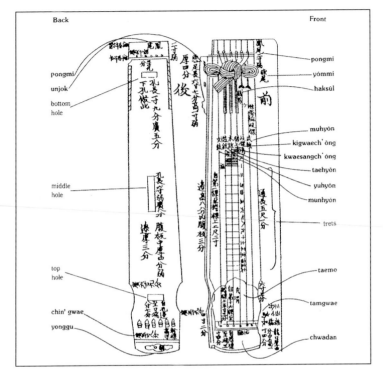

3.2 The depiction of *kŏmun'go* in the treatise *Akhak kwebŏm*.

A famous zither master and singer make music together:
Im Chŏngch'ŏl knows the zither well;
The strings run across a body of fine paulownia and
By moving the bridges of this splendid instrument and tuning
    the strings
How wonderful is the sound! Its slow prelude is long
    and melancholy.

Partly due to this aristocratic heritage, but ignoring the origin site of the legend, the *kŏmun'go* has been dropped in North Korea. In Seoul, its status has regularly been confirmed. Indeed, several former directors of the court institute and senior scholars were trained as *kŏmun'go* players.

The *kŏmun'go* is a six-string half-tube zither (H/S 312.22.6), plucked with a pencil-shaped bamboo stick (*sultae* or *shi*). It has 16 perpendicularly fixed frets (*kwae*) beneath the inner strings and three movable bridges (properly *chu*, but now more usually known as *kirŏgi pal*) under the outer strings. The twisted silk strings vary in thickness and are plucked above a leather cover, the *taemo* ('hawksbill') or *sasŭm* ('deer'). The front board is again a convex and burnished piece of old paulownia, and the sides and back are usually chestnut. The strings are held in a similar way to those of the *kayagŭm*, with pegs at the top and cords below, but they are much thicker. Symbolism, akin to that of the Japanese *koto*, is enshrined in the instrument. A *yonggu* ('dragon's mouth') at the top end is matched by small glued feet, *unjok* ('cloud legs'), at the base. The strings are anchored to cords that are tied in a way said to resemble a phoenix tail (*pongmi*). The outer strings are known as *munhyŏn* (civil string) and *muhyŏn* (army string). Only strings 2 and 3, *yuhyŏn* (played string) and *taehyŏn* (big string), provide the melodies. The other strings are labelled *kwaesangch'ŏng* (clear tone above bridge) and *kwaehach'ŏng* (clear tone below bridge; formerly *kigwaech'ŏng*). In court use the open strings are commonly tuned E^b, A^b, D^b, B^b, B^b, $B^{b'}$, giving a range up to $b^{b'}$ at the sixteenth fret (Fig. 3.3). A *sanjo* version of the instrument exists, similar to the court version in construction but a little shorter (approximately 140cm rather than 150cm long).

The *kŏmun'go* produces a sound that mixes percussion and melody. The stick, held in the right hand, deliberately strikes the soundboard and creates accent through rapid movements across several strings. The strings are loose,

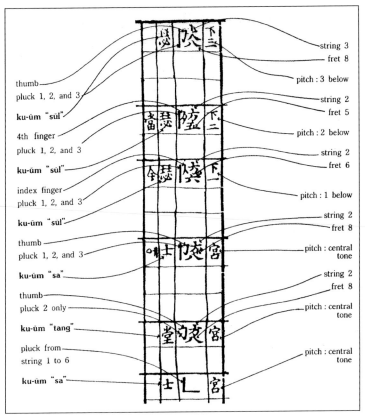

3.3 A sample of tablature for the *kŏmun'go*, annotated from *Kŭm hapchabo*. Read from top to bottom, adding together all the information (for example, 'play string 3 with thumb at fret 8, but pluck all of strings 1, 2, and 3').

and resonance quickly fades. The left hand, with the ring finger anchored on string 2, both stops strings at a fret to generate the appropriate pitch and pushes the strings across a given fret to produce ornaments and to raise the pitch.

A further zither, the *ajaeng*, has also disappeared in North Korea in recent years. The sound of the court *ajaeng* is particularly curious and is created by moving a stick of rosined forsythia wood across the strings. This practice maintains an old tradition in China, where the *yazheng* (*ya* = creak; *zheng* = zither) had been in use at least by the eighth century AD. The court *ajaeng* is a bowed half-tube zither (H/S 312.22.71) with movable bridges and with seven thick silk strings tuned to cover a narrow range of a 9th, normally A^b–b^b. In Koryŏ times it was labelled a *tangak* instrument, but by the time of *Akhak kwebŏm* it was played in some *hyangak* ensembles. More recently, a folk version has evolved. This has an additional string, a second paulownia soundboard, and is played across a much wider range (F–$b^{b'}$) with the aid of a cello bow. This version is particularly versatile: it can become a *kayagŭm* when plucked, obviating the need to employ expensive extra musicians, and when bowed can create a number of theatrical effects.

Three zithers imported from China for use in court rituals are preserved (all H/S 312.22.5). One, the seven-string lacquered *kŭm*, is a copy of a Chinese *qin*. The others share the paulownia-based construction of the *kŏmun'go* and *ajaeng*. The 25-string *sŭl* is tuned to a chromatic scale in which string 13 remains mute. Unique amongst Korean zithers, it has a painted paulownia soundboard decorated with a bird motif. Four 15-string *taejaeng* were imported from China in 1114, and 42 *sŭl* and 73 *kŭm* arrived in 1116. Koreans soon lost the playing techniques of all three and, although one or two continued to be placed in the orchestra for the rite to Confucius, they only began to be widely heard again in the 1970s.

The *haegŭm* also came to Korea from China, but its name appears to be a corruption of a tribe's name from the Xinjiang region of Chinese Central Asia. First mentioned in Korea in *Hallim pyŏlgok*, a thirteenth-century song, the *haegŭm*, according to *Akhak kwebŏm*, is alone amongst instruments in using all eight materials in the *p'al ŭm* classification. In the fifteenth century, then, it seems that it had a bamboo resonator and neck, frontal wooden pegs, a metal base plate, silk strings, a gourd bridge, a leather handpiece to the bow, rosin on the bow, and crushed stone coating the inside of the resonator. Today, hardwoods tend to replace bamboo, and the soundboard is paulownia. *Haegŭm* were widely used, not least since they were considered to bind the sustained nature of wind instruments to the fast decay of zither tones. In *Yŏngsan hoesang*, therefore, the *haegŭm* both echoes the *kŏmun'go* and doubles the *p'iri*. *Haegŭm* have played *tangak* and *hyangak* pieces and were until recently common in shamanistic ritual ensembles.

The *haegŭm*, as it survives in South Korea, remains a two-string spiked fiddle (H/S 321.313.7)(Plate 12). It has counterparts throughout the Muslim world and in the Minnan and Chaozhou *erxian*, the Han Chinese *erhu*, the Vietnamese *dan nhi* and *dan co*, and the Japanese *kokyu*. Few modifications have been made to the design in Korea, hence it retains a peculiar nasal sound quality and is notoriously difficult to play. The musician sits on the floor, supporting the base of the resonator by the right foot above the left knee. The bow is tensed manually and threads between the strings. The strings are tuned a fifth apart (Fig. 3.4). There is no finger-board, so pitching is achieved in mid-air, discouraging any sense of precisely tuned, steady pitches (Fig. 3.5). There are four basic finger positions, and strings are also pulled in towards the neck, tightening them to raise the pitch. The normal range is two octaves, a^b–$a^{b''}$.

In North Korea, the *haegŭm* has been redesigned (Plate 13). The soundboard is now softwood of greater strength than paulownia. The soundbox is squashed flat, a soundpost connects its belly to its back, and there are two frontal

3.4 A *haegŭm* fiddle score for *Seryŏngsan*, the first movement of the chamber suite *Yŏngsan hoesang*, written in *chŏngganbo* notation by Kim Kisu. *Chŏngganbo*, read from right to left and top to bottom, is a Korean mensural notation system with Sino-Korean pitch indicators; it has been in use since the fifteenth century.

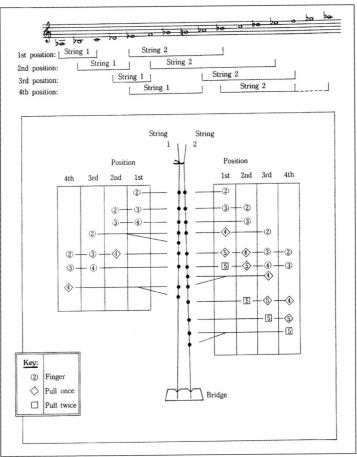

3.5 A fingering chart for the traditional *haegŭm* in court music, showing four positions. To reach certain pitches, the two strings must be manually pulled towards the neck.

soundholes, all as in Western violins. The bow, tensed mechanically, is likewise borrowed, and passes over—not between—four metal strings. The strings are attached to lateral pegs. They run over a fingerboard, hence pitches can be precisely tuned. The result is less acoustic damping, because of the resonant property of the soundbox, the loss of the deadening inner coating of earth, and since the contact between finger and string is mediated by pressing on a solid board.

Just as there are four Western string instruments, there are now four *haegŭm* (Fig. 3.6). The three smaller versions, *so haegŭm*, *chung haegŭm*, and *tae haegŭm*, have strings tuned in fifths, each sounding a tone beneath their violin, viola, and cello equivalents; each instrument provides a three-octave range: f–g‴, B^b–c‴, and $B^{b'}$–c″, respectively. The largest version, *chŏ haegŭm*, is tuned in fourths like the double-bass to give a range of D´–b^{b'}. The playing position for all four versions has been altered. The musicians no longer sit on the floor, but on a chair. The two smaller instruments are supported on the lap, unlike the chin support of violins but not far removed from seventeenth-century Western viols, Moroccan violins, and the contemporary Chinese *erhu*. The two larger instruments stand on the floor with the aid of a spike, like the Western cello and bass.

Three long-necked lutes (H/S 321.321.6) are preserved at the court institute in Seoul. Although all are obsolete, efforts have begun to reintroduce them into some ensembles. The four-string *tang pip'a* has a long neck bent back at the pegbox, four large frets on the neck, and eight thin frets on the soundboard. It was plucked with a fan-shaped wooden plectrum (*palmok*) or three artificial nails (*kajogak*). Included in Huizong's 1116 gift, it became part of the

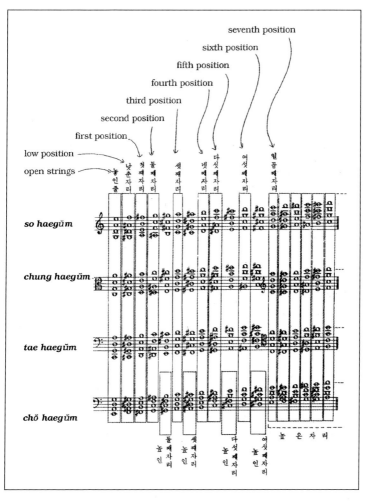

3.6 North Korean fingering systems for the four 'improved' *haegŭm*.

ensemble for *tangak* pieces. The *hyang pip'a* has a longer history. It was well-established as the *ohyŏn pip'a* in Koguryŏ and was absorbed into the standard Shilla court ensemble.

It has a straight neck, five strings and, by the time of *Akhak kwebŏm*, it had 10 wooden frets glued to the soundboard. Korean literati played the instrument until the Japanese colonial period. The third lute is the 4-string *wŏlgŭm*. The term *wŏl* means 'moon' and refers to the instrument's round soundbox. This lute was called *yuanxian* in Chinese antiquity, likely after Yuan Xian, one of the Seven Sages of the Bamboo Grove. The *wŏlgŭm* was present from at least the fourth century in Koguryŏ, since it is depicted in tombs such as those at Anak, Changchuan, and Tongguo (on the Manchurian bank of the Yalu River). The playing technique given for it in *Akhak kwebŏm* is similar to that for the *tang pip'a*, and the treatise describes 13 frets, 12 of which are on the neck. It was in use until the nineteenth century and, because of its association with Koguryŏ, this appears to be the only lute still described in North Korean texts.

Three harps preserved in Seoul were brought from Beijing in 1937 by Ham Hwajin (1889–1948), a performer and theoretician who rose to become director of the court music institute. In Korea, the harps appear in tomb murals and old court documents, but all have long been obsolete. The vertical harp, *sugonghu* (H/S 322.21.5), has 21 strings above a soundbox, while the arched harp, *wagonghu* (H/S 322.11.5), has 13 strings and an integral soundbox. Evidence for their use in Korea is sketchy, based on Sui dynasty records and a few faded tomb paintings. The vertical harp *sogonghu*, with 13 strings but no soundbox, may have more claim to a Korean identity. It is depicted in a relief on a bell dated to 721 AD at Sangwŏn temple in Kangwŏn province. And, labelled as if imported from Paekche, two examples are preserved at the Shösöin repository.

A dulcimer, the *yanggŭm* (H/S 314.122.4), was likely brought to Korea in the late eighteenth century. Several centuries earlier, Christian missionaries had imported it to China, where it is known as the *yangqin*. An 1817 Korean score book, giving the alternative name *kurach'ŏlsa kŭm*, suggests European origins for the instrument. The *yanggŭm* is flat and trapezoidal, and in South Korea is struck with a single bamboo beater. In ensemble, it merely strikes out the main melodic contour. North Korean players, to achieve a fluency akin to Central European dulcimer players, now use two beaters. In the South it is placed on its case and played on the floor; in the North it is raised on a trestle. The old structure features choirs of seven sets of four metal strings. These pass over two bridges that alternate raised edges with gaps. One choir passes from pegs on the left over the raised edges of a first bridge, through the gaps of a second bridge to pins at the right. The other choir does the same in reverse. Strings can be tuned on both sides of the raised bridge, and this gives a potential 28 pitches. Twenty-one are actually tuned to give a total range e^b–$a^{b'''}$. The North Korean version has an expanded range, c–g'''.

This brings us to one final string instrument, the *ongnyugŭm* (H/S 314.122.5)(Plate 14). Named after a river site near P'yŏngyang, this is a box zither with a single row of nylon strings. Development of this instrument began in North Korea in 1973, after Kim Jong Il, a longstanding supporter of the arts and son of Kim Il Sung, decreed that instruments should be modernized to compete with Western music. Northern scholars describe it as a successor to the obsolete harps, but the *ongnyugŭm* has a much more complex heritage. The most recent version has 32 strings and is tuned diatonically to give a maximum range C–$g^{\#''''}$. It incorporates the shape of the *yanggŭm* and playing techniques derived directly from the *kayagŭm*. A row of bridges also resemble the moveable *anjok* of the *kayagŭm*, but they are fixed in a manner not dissimilar to the rows of bridges on many French and Flemish dulcimers. The Western orchestral harp appears to have been influential: colour-coded strings mark fifths and octaves and a similar double-action pedal mechanism operates on the strings beyond the bridges. The seven pedals work on seven diatonic pitches and are connected by a pulley mechanism to a rotating triskele above the soundboard. There are three positions: '0' (standard), where one arm of the triskele stops the string at a small second bridge; '-' (flat), where the triskele arms are raised away from the strings so that the string length increases back to a third bridge; and '+' (sharp), where a second arm of the triskele stops the string just behind the main bridge. (The harp sequence is different: -, 0, +.)

In terms of sound capability, the *ongnyugŭm* comes closest amongst North Korean developments to matching the indigenous with Western music. Some common *kayagŭm* playing techniques remain, such as vibrato and a few ornaments associated with sudden pitch alteration. Other techniques such as tremolo, which had no place in old music, are now common and seem to reflect the development of European, Middle Eastern, and contemporary Chinese dulcimers. Other techniques capitalize on the possibilities for bright glissandi and harmonic in-fills beneath the melody. The *ongnyugŭm* has now spread beyond North Korea: it can be found amongst the Korean community in China's Jilin province, and via Jilin has recently reached South Korea.

4

Wind Instruments

KING SHINMUN (r.681–92) heard that a mountain was float-
ing in the Eastern Sea near Kamŭn temple, a temple he
had founded. An astrologer, Kim Ch'unjil, divined that the
king's father had returned as a dragon along with Kim
Yushin, a famous general who had died a decade before.
Together, the astrologer said, they wished to give the king
a treasure to protect the realm. A servant sent to look at
the mountain reported that a bamboo plant growing on the
peak split into two during daylight but fused as a single
shoot each night. At noon the next day, the bamboo fused
and a great storm arose that left the skies dark for a week.
The king crossed to the mountain and was instructed by
the dragon to cut the bamboo. A flute was made from the
bamboo and, whenever this was played, enemies retreated,
illnesses were cured, rain came after drought, and the sea
remained calm.

This legend is recorded in *Samguk yusa* to account for
the invention of Korea's best-loved wind instrument, the
large transverse flute *taegŭm* (H/S 421.121.12, with the
addition of an integral sympathetic resonator)(Plate 15). The
legend ends by ascribing a special name to the instrument:
the *manman p'ap'ashik chŏk*, the 'flute to calm 100 million waves' (many Koreans know it as the '10,000 wave'
manp'ashik chŏk). Recent excavations at the site of Kamŭn
temple revealed stone carvings of musicians, including a
deva playing a transverse flute. This flute appears slender,
more like the Chinese *hengdi* than today's *taegŭm*. The
Korean flute is made from a length of glorious yellow bamboo (*hwang chuk*) with prominent nodes. Good instruments
contain five years' growth of bamboo and have ducts

running along either side between nodes that mark where a branch grew. The top is sealed with wax and has a large blowing hole (*ch'wi kong*). Six finger holes (*chi kong*), spread more or less equidistantly but frustratingly further apart than most musicians find comfortable, are cut beneath a covered oval hole (*ch'ŏng kong*). Two or more 'Big Dipper' holes (*ch'ilsŏng kong*), drilled in part for decoration, finish the lower part of the tube to define the sounding length.

The *taegŭm* was one of three flutes in the Unified Shilla *samhyŏn samjuk* ensemble. The other two, *chunggŭm* and *sogŭm*, are similar but shorter and, although now absent in court ensembles, can occasionally still be bought in local markets. The *taegŭm*, alone, has a mirliton: a tissue (*kaltae*) cut from bamboo or reed that can be exposed to produce a unique and characteristic buzzing effect. This covers the oval hole and makes the *taegŭm* distinct in Korea, although comparable transverse flutes exist in both Japan and China. The Japanese *ryuteki* is more elaborate than is the *taegŭm*, with a body wrapped in twine or cherry bark, but it is smaller than the *taegŭm* and, curiously, is classified separately from the *komabue* flute, an instrument that supposedly came from Korea. The Chinese *di* first came to Koguryŏ as the *hoengjŏk*, but by the time of the Tang dynasty in the seventh to tenth centuries the Chinese instrument had seven finger holes. This version became the Korean *tangjŏk*, an instrument which now survives in some court music such as the wind ensemble piece *Sujech'ŏn* (Life under clear skies) and is preserved across the Eastern Sea as the Japanese *oteki*. By the time of the Ming dynasty in the fourteenth to seventeenth centuries, the favoured Chinese configuration was six finger holes and a mirliton. It may be supposed, then, that considerable interchange took place between the Korean and Chinese instruments.

The court *taegŭm*, around 80–85cm long, has a range

b^b–$e^{b'''}$. Vibrato is produced by bobbing the head up and down, and considerable pitch adjustment can be made by altering the embouchure across the large blowing hole. *Akhak kwebŏm* confined the *taegŭm* to the indigenous *hyangak*, but it also plays in Chinese-originating *tangak* pieces such as *Nagyangch'un*. It is common in literati-based *chŏngak*, such as in the suite *Yŏngsan hoesang* and in the accompaniment to song repertories. Indeed, its most famous piece is *Ch'ŏngsŏnggok* (also known as *Ch'ŏngsŏng chajin hanip*), a solo extracted from a *kagok* lyric song. Instruments for folk music, slightly shorter, are tuned about a tone higher. They are now popular for *sanjo*, and once featured in shaman ritual ensembles. Curious legends surround the famous shaman who created *taegŭm sanjo*, Pak Chonggi (1879–1939). It is said that while he mourned for his father, confined in an appropriate small shrine to show filial piety, he received a vision telling his family where to find bamboo with which to make a special instrument. When he played this flute, birds settled on his shoulders. And he is said to have died with the instrument attached to his lips: a student saw blood dripping from the 'Big Dipper' holes.

Both versions of the *taegŭm* have three distinct ranges: low (*yat'ŭn tan*); medium, overblown at the octave (*chunggan tan*); and high, overblown at the 12th (*nop'ŭn tan*). Moreover, the mirliton can be adjusted to enhance three specified tone colours: the clear and highly vibrated soft *chŏ ch'wi*, the elegant and strident *p'yŏng ch'wi*, and the triumphant *yŏk ch'wi*. The drive to 'improve' instruments in North Korea has led to the creation of three new versions. All three abandon bamboo in favour of smooth hardwood bodies. Although said to recreate the Unified Shilla ensemble, this is spurious, since they actually take parallel roles to the concert, alto, and bass flutes of a Western orchestra. All three adopt the structure of Western flutes, with similar shapes and nickel-plated simple-system key-work. In keeping with politics, however, a vernacular name for them is preferred: *chŏttae*.

The *tanso* (H/S 421.111.12)(Plate 16), in South Korea a simple end-blown notched pipe, is similar to the longer Chinese *xiao* (in fact, the Sino-Korean characters are shared with the Han Chinese *duanxiao*). The Japanese *shakuhachi* is much larger, but shares a common layout of four anterior finger holes and a posterior thumb hole. It is made from the same wood, *ojuk*, old and dark bamboo (in Japanese, *odake*). The base of both instruments flares out, since it is cut from the root bulb. Old jade examples have been discovered and today plastic seems unfortunately to be gaining in popularity. The *tanso* is considered an easy instrument to play, suitable for school use, and an appropriate training instrument to be mastered before a student progresses to the majestic *taegŭm* (Fig. 4.1).

The 'improved' North Korean version shares the *chŏttae* construction, with a two-piece hardwood body. Keywork covers five holes in addition to six finger holes. The old range has been increased from a normative $g^{b\prime}$–$g^{b\prime\prime\prime}$ to $a^{b\prime}$–$f^{\prime\prime\prime\prime}$. The instrument can now imitate pieces from the old *taegŭm* repertory, while revisions generate the ability to work in diatonic rather than the old pentatonic modes. And, as with the old *taegŭm*, three registers are distinguished, now called in a rather less colourful manner low (*najŭn sori mok*), middle (*kaunde sori mok*), and high (*nop'ŭn sori mok*).

Texts state that King Sunjo (r.1801–34) imported the *tanso* to Korea. While some scholars suggest that these texts document its first appearance on the peninsula, all we should conclude is that the instrument had not been used in court ensembles before this time. The *tanso* is a simple instrument, common in many parts of the world, and it could well have been present amongst folk musicians. After all,

local Koreans still tend to call any blowing instrument a
p'iri, so the terms *tanso* and *taegŭm* would probably not
have registered in accounts of life in the countryside. Players
of the old *tanso* are renowned for their ornamentation of
melodies, with a catalogue of complex pre-tone and after-
tone decorations. Less vibrato was possible than on the
taegŭm, a function of the limited potential for lip move-

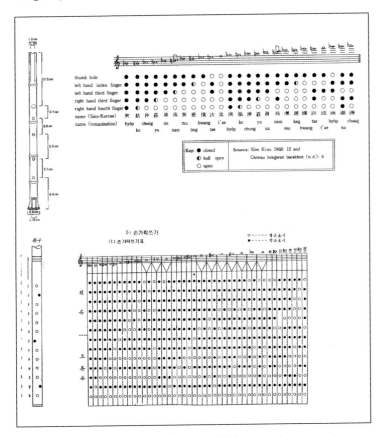

4.1 Traditional (*chŏnt'ong*) and 'improved' (*kaeryang*) *tanso* tuning systems.

ment on the small mouthpiece. North Korea's *tanso*, however, is played with increased vibrato coupled with much less complex ornamentation. The focus has moved from the elaboration of single tones to passing tones and approach tones that enhance a sequential melody.

The 40cm long *tanso* is related to the larger, 60–65cm *t'ungso* (Fig. 4.2). The latter, also known as the *t'ongso* or

4.2 An unorthodox form of the *t'ungso*, as played to accompany the mask dance, *Pukch'ŏng saja norŭm*. The music and dance originated in the north but are now preserved in South Korea as Intangible Cultural Asset No. 15.

t'ungae, once played in the orchestra at the Rite to Royal Ancestors, had six finger holes. *Akhak kwebŏm* attributed to it a range of just over two octaves, but rural *t'ungso* lack any standard form. One, in a mask drama, *Pukch'ŏng saja norŭm*, that originated in what is now North Korea,

4.3 The *chi*.

has just four finger holes beneath a mirliton (players call the mirliton itself the *t'ungae*).

Three further flute types arrived from China in 1116 and are retained only for the Rite to Confucius. All three are made from yellow bamboo. One, the *chi* (H/S 421.121.22) (Fig. 4.3), may have been present in Korea as long ago as during the Paekche period. It is transverse, uses old dark wood, and has a peculiar shape featuring a raised vertical mouthpiece and five finger holes, the first of which is placed on the side for the left thumb. A cross-shaped opening at the base is also stopped to give a total but narrow range of c′–e♭″. The other two, the *yak* and *chŏk* (both H/S 421.111.12), are vertical flutes made from simple tubes. The *yak* has three finger holes and a range of a seventh, c–b, and the *chŏk* has five finger holes and a posterior thumb hole producing a tenth range one octave lower than the *chi*, c–e♭′.

Another instrument, the panpipes, *so* (H/S 421.112.2), is also confined to the Rite to Confucius and, due to its singularly ritual use, has not changed appreciably from the version described in the *Akhak kwebŏm*. *So* were received as gifts from the Chinese court in 1114, 1116, and again in 1406. Sixteen notched bamboo pipes, encompassed and held in a wooden frame said to resemble the unfolded wings of a phoenix, are arranged in a row fanning outwards from the shortest (high pitch) to the longest (low pitch) at each end.

Folded phoenix wings provide the shape of the mouthorgan, the *saenghwang* (H/S 412.132), as well. Seventeen slender pipes project upwards from a chest now made from metal or wood. Each pipe has a finger hole near its base and is slit near the top, and 16 have internal free metal reeds. The pipes sound only when the finger hole is closed, but one pipe is mute. Their range is $e^{b'}$ to c'''.

Huizong sent 10 *saenghwang* to Korea in 1114 and 80 in 1116. Two more arrived from the Ming emperor Yongle in 1406, but the instrument was known to be in use even earlier than these gifts. Chinese sources attest to its use in Paekche, and a stone relief of the Unified Shilla era and a bell (cast in 725) at Sangwŏn temple show devas playing it. There is no record of the *saenghwang* ever being made in Korea; in 1657 and at other times examples were purchased in China. Thus, Chinese and Japanese instruments differ only marginally from those found in Korea, in the number of mute pipes and in the manner of playing. Today, the *saenghwang* has a limited repertory confined to state rituals, a single duet with the *tanso* called *Chajin hanip* or *Seryongŭm*, and a handful of contemporary compositions.

A tear-shaped globular ocarina, the *hun* (H/S 421.221.42) is even more limited in its use, playing in the Rite to

Confucius and one or two new pieces. Seventy-two *hun* were brought from China in the twelfth century although they, too, were known earlier on the peninsula. As in China, the instrument is made from baked clay with a blowing hole at its apex, two posterior thumb holes, and three anterior finger holes. It is no more than 9cm in height and diameter. Held in cupped hands, a single octave's 12 chromatic pitches can be produced, although some are weak since they are produced by partially covering holes. *Akhak kwebŏm* remarks on the difficulty of producing good instruments: the solution it gives is to make a batch and throw away all but the best.

Shamans say that one instrument attracts the spirits better than any other. This is the oboe called *p'iri* (Plate 17). To many in the countryside, the *p'iri* most closely amongst all instruments imitates the human voice. It is the archetypal folk instrument, and a number of variants exist, ranging from plastic tubes through to *hodŭgi* (stripped-bark pipes) and *ch'ojŏk* (the leaf). Let us consider the latter first: A single piece of bark detached from its core is typical of the many different *hodŭgi*. These were often produced by children and were common until about 20 years ago. Some still exist as little more than toys in South Korea, although I saw one old woman in P'yŏngyang in 1992 hawking similar instruments constructed from hollow stems. There are several distinct types of *ch'ojŏk* in country districts; they are called *ch'ogŭm*, *ch'aegŭm*, and so on. Local performers say that leaves of mandarin and citron trees, folded along one edge to create a double reed, are best. The sound is not unlike that European stand-by, the comb and paper. A second and more curious variant, a leaf rolled into a tube, is described in *Akhak kwebŏm.*

The *p'iri* itself is a small pipe normally constructed from a length of bamboo with a very large, separate, shaved

51

double reed (*kaltae*). The Chinese *guan* and the Japanese *hichiriki* are related instruments. Three traditional versions are still used in South Korea. Two, the *hyang p'iri* (indigenous oboe; also known as *tae p'iri* and *sagwan*)(Plate 18) and *se p'iri* (slender oboe), are cylindrical pipes about 25cm long with eight finger holes (H/S 422.111.2). Both employ a basic range of a 10th, ascending from a^b in the court and b^b in common folk usage with no overblowing. The range can be extended upwards by about a fourth by altering the lip pressure on the reed.

Hyang p'iri feature as a major, strident instrument in court ensembles such as that for *Sujech'ŏn* and the 'string' version of *Yŏngsan hoesang*. *Hyang p'iri* are also, as their name indicates, the preferred folk and *sanjo* instrument. Oboes presumed similar to the *hyang p'iri* were part of the Koguryŏ ensembles that played at the Chinese Sui court in the sixth century, but they are rarely depicted in tomb paintings and references to them have not been found inscribed on artefacts. Ch'oe Ch'iwŏn (b.857), a Shilla-era scholar who spent many years studying in Tang China, stated that they were integral to the five dramatic genres of Shilla culture. *Se p'iri* produce a thinner, softer sound than do *hyang p'iri*, and they are ideally suited for accompanying song genres such as *kagok* lyric songs.

The third version of the *p'iri* is still used in the remnants of *tangak* and *hyangak* court repertories. This is the *tang p'iri* (Chinese oboe), constructed from a slightly conical tube of old and dark bamboo with prominent nodes (H/S 422.112.2). Some overblowing is used to give a current potential range c´–a˝. Twenty arrived, listed as *p'illyul*, courtesy of Huizong in 1114. These had seven anterior finger holes and two thumb holes. The lower thumb hole has now disappeared; King Sejong is credited with 'improving' the instrument, arguing that this hole was redundant.

Further 'improvements' had to wait a few centuries until the emergence of a post-war regime in North Korea. The three oboes now used in P'yŏngyang—the *so p'iri* (small oboe), *tae p'iri* (large oboe), and *chŏ p'iri* (bass oboe)—reflect, like the three 'improved' transverse flutes, the exigencies of creating a complete texture to match that of Western orchestras. All three retain oversize bamboo double reeds. The *so p'iri* is simply an updated version of the *hyang p'iri*, but with a birch or rosewood cylindrical tube to which the player applies overblowing to extend the narrow range to two octaves (c′–d‴). The *tae p'iri* and *chŏ p'iri* are considerably modified to provide equivalents to orchestral bassoons and contra-bassoons. The keywork on both is superficially similar to that of a Boehm clarinet; the thumb support and fingering system on the *tae p'iri* closely match an orchestral clarinet, and the *chŏ p'iri* resembles the bass clarinet. The *tae p'iri* has an extended cylindrical hardwood body with a conical top section to give an extended range c–b♭″. The *chŏ p'iri* doubles the tube back on itself, thereby lowering the sound by an octave.

The three final wind instrument types had antecedents on Asian battlefields. They are loud, and all play in the colourful and lively processional *Taech'wit'a*. The *nabal* (H/S 423.121.12), a straight trumpet made of interlocking lengths of brass tube, sounds a simple harmonic series. Similar to the Chinese *laba*, and today resembling what the *Akhak kwebŏm* described as a *taegak*, it is also common amongst folk bands, where it signals the beginning of a performance. The *nagak* (H/S 423.111.2), with alternative names such as *na* and *sora*, belongs to that curious type of instrument—conch shells—found from Ancient

Greece to Melanesia. In Korea it sounds just a single tone; the shell has no standard size and, apart from a mouthpiece, is not modified with, for instance, a fingerhole. The Korean version was present from Koryŏ times, and *Akhak kwebŏm* says that it should be placed in front of dancers at the Rite to Royal Ancestors. It, however, no longer plays a part in that rite, unlike the final wind instrument, the *t'aep'yŏngso* (H/S 422.112.2)(Plate 19), which plays in three sections of it.

The *t'aep'yŏngso* is a double-reed shawm. Similar instruments moved from Central Asia, westwards as far as North Africa and eastwards with Chinese and Indian traders. The common Chinese name, *suona*, suggests Middle Eastern roots, but an alternative name common in Korea, *hojŏk* (in Chinese, *hoejok*), specifically refers to tribes of the Xinjiang region in north-west China. Koreans believe it arrived in Koryŏ times, but it is first mentioned only much later, as an instrument specifically for *tangak*, in Sŏng Hyŏn's *Akhak kwebŏm*. Today, as the *saenap* (or *soaenap*) and *nallari*, it is used to improvise melodies in many folk bands. In South Korea, the conical tube is still made from Chinese date (jujube), with seven finger holes and a posterior thumb hole. A small bamboo double reed (or, for practice, a short plastic straw) sits atop a short metal pipe, and a metal bell completes the base. In the South, it is considered a difficult and temperamental instrument to play. This is not the case in North Korea, where an 'improved' *chang saenap* boasts a larger reed similar to the Western oboe, a longer, smooth sandalwood body, and simple-system keywork. The *chang saenap* expands the old range, from a normative $a^{b\prime}$–$e^{b\prime\prime\prime}$ to a chromatic $c\prime$–$f^{\#\prime\prime\prime\prime}$. It boasts a repertory based around updated folk melodies, and often replaces the *so p'iri* as the Western oboe equivalent, in orchestral ensembles.

5

Percussion Instruments

In Korea, rhythm is a vital element of music. Regularly repeating patterns, rhythmic cycles known as *changdan* (*chang* = long; *tan/dan* = short), feature in virtually all court and folk genres. *Changdan* prescribe a downbeat, the *hap changdan* or *wŏnbak*, on which all musicians play together, and points of accent that extend the upbeat back into the cycle. *Changdan* are associated with model patterns that, almost like miniature versions of the melodic Javanese *balungan* or Indian raga, function as an internal code to provide the basis for variation and development. Hemiola and syncopation are well developed, cutting across points of accent but rarely threatening the downbeat. Whereas melody has been paramount in the Western canon, and in Western musical thought ever since the rhythmic modes of the twelfth-century Notre Dame school, rhythm is the defining feature of much Korean music. This is particularly the case with folk music. Folk bands play pure rhythm, with melodic improvisation offering an occasional gloss to brighten the texture. *Sanjo* movements and *p'ansori* songs are described in terms of the *changdan*, so that *chinyangjo* is a slow, emotionally charged 18/8 pattern, *chungmori* an everyday walking-paced 12/4, and *chajinmori* a fast and agitated 12/8. Many *changdan* give rise to specific melodic palettes: melodic development arises from the rhythmic structure.

Translate *changdan* to instruments and it is apparent that drums will be quintessential. One, the *changgo*, a double-headed barrel drum (H/S 211.242.1) (Plate 20), is ubiquitous in most genres. Some historical sources refer to the *changgo* as a *seyogo*, 'narrow waisted drum', and this term, together with an additional name for the body, *chorongmok*, reiterate the characteristic hourglass shape. Wooden bodies are most common, turned on a lathe from a single piece of light and resonant paulownia wood. Pottery bodies, cast from one piece or made from two interlocking bowls, also exist. Indeed, *Akhak kwebŏm* cites a thirteenth-century source, the *Wenxian tonggao*, as evidence that ancient Chinese drums were made with both pottery and wood bodies. Court instruments are large and may be painted red, the royal colour. Size seems to reflect use: they are placed on the ground and played while seated. Folk instruments need to be lighter, since they are slung over the shoulders, resting at the waist, and can be used in processions and dances. The bodies of these are rarely painted, although oil or varnish is used to enhance the grain and to protect the wood.

Akhak kwebŏm states that the best skins (*p'yŏn*) are made from horses. Today, the considerable expense this would involve means that cow, goat, or pigskin usually suffices. Such skins are adequate on drums used for accompaniment, where the left head is struck by the hand to give a low thud. The right head is always tighter and thinner, and it is struck on its circumference with a thin whip-like stick known as the *yŏl ch'ae* to produce a higher relative pitch. Folk bands, however, now use a second stick. This is a mallet with flexible bamboo stem known as the *kunggul ch'ae* or *k'ung ch'ae*. Bands most often play outdoors, and the mallet is ideal to produce greater volume. It also lends itself to the creation of virtuosic patterns. As a result, the folk *changgo* is associated with complex generic solo pieces such as *sŏl changgo* and *changgo nori*, played by brawny farmers in the countryside or as part of the floor shows given by young, ever-smiling girls in Seoul's international hotels. The mallet stick attacks the heads with force, while the whip-like stick, to match, moves from the circumference to the centre of the head. Greater resilience is required of these heads than on court instruments, hence dogskin commonly substitutes for cheaper materials that would tend to break frequently.

The two heads are not directly attached to the body. Instead, each overlaps the circumference of the bowl and is stretched around a metal ring. Cords known as *chihongsa* attach to the rings to lace the heads together. Tension is increased by tightening leather or plastic V-shaped thongs (*karak chi* or *ch'uksu*) over the cords. In South Korea, although the performance style has not changed, different materials have recently been promoted for *changgo* bodies. Plastic interlocking bowls are made by the Arirang Company in Seoul, and alloy bowls can be bought in Chŏlla and Ch'ungch'ŏng provincial markets. In North Korea, two developments have occurred. First, the structure of *changdan* has been undermined as greater emphasis has been placed on metrical music. Second, to facilitate the use of *changgo* in mixed ensembles and light music bands, a new drum kit has evolved which includes pedalled bass *changgo*, bongo-*changgo*, and nearly all possible variants in between (Fig. 5.1).

5.1 A *changgo* drum kit developed in North Korea.

A second drum, the *puk* (Plate 21), provides the accompaniment to *p'ansori* and, often, to compositions of one *kayagŭm sanjo* school, that of Ch'oe Oksan. The use of the *puk* in the latter may reflect a rumoured love affair between the asset-holder Ham Tongjŏngwŏl and the great *p'ansori* drummer Kim Myŏnghwan (1913–88). The *puk* is a shallow double-headed barrel drum. The body was once made from a single trunk but, given the scarcity of large trees in Korea, now tends to comprise interlocking slats. On *p'ansori* instruments, the body may be covered in skin, with cow or pigskin heads nailed to the body (H/S 211.222.7). The heads are held by leather thongs on folk instruments (H/S 211.222.8)(Plate 22). In *p'ansori*, a single smooth hardwood stick is employed, punctuating a singer's phrases and keeping the *changdan* by striking both one skin and the wooden body. Folk musicians variously employ a single stick, a stick and the hand, and two sticks in Miryang (Kyŏngsang province, south-east) and Chindo (Chŏlla province, south-west). For *p'ansori*, the *puk* is placed in front of the seated players; in folkbands it is slung over the shoulder. The music produced never reaches the complexity of *changgo* rhythms: a clue to why is the dull sound of its onomatopoeic name. A more decorated version of the *puk*, the *yonggo*, is hung at the waist in the court processional, *Taech'wit'a*, and is played on the upper skin with two sticks.

Folk bands have long been a common sight and sound in the Korean countryside. Many would suggest military origins for their music, claiming that drums were used to sound attacks and gongs the retreat on Chinese battlefields. Indeed, in 1737 a government emissary discovered what he presumed to be 'military' banners at Puan in North Chŏlla province. The court was distraught: could a rebellion be brewing? A false alarm was soon called, when King Yŏngjo (r.1725–76) was reassured by his agents: 'There are some farmers who aren't active while everyone else works hard...they sound metallic gongs to cheer the workers up' (*Yŏngjo shillok* [Annals], Vol. 47).

In 1906, the *Report on Agricultural Products of Korea* described novel Korean farming methods to an American audience:

We witnessed that music is played and singing is done to encourage the weeding work. They raise a banner on which is written 'Farming is the basis of the world'. Walking around the countryside in the weeding season, one hears the sound of gongs. Particularly when they feel tired after a day of hard toil, some farmers change...from weeding to musical instruments and start playing exciting strains for the workers.

In folk bands, the *changgo* and *puk* are led by small and large gongs (H/S 111.241.1)(Plate 23). Musicians have given them onomatopoeic names: *kkwaenggwari*, *kkwaengma*, and so on for the small instrument; *ching*, *kŭmjing*, and so on for the large gong. The small gong, held by the left hand, played with a beater, and damped with fingers on the back of the body, is the instrument of a band leader (Plate 24). He is typically known as the *sangsoe*, 'leading iron'. He sounds the model *changdan* for all to hear and signals changes in rhythm. The large gong strikes accents with a soft, padded beater. Due to its resonance, musicians agree that the large gong is vital: it keeps the band in time. The whip-like stick of the *changgo* imitates small gong patterns, while the mallet stick echoes large gong strikes; the *puk* elaborates on what the large gong plays.

A further drum is also frequently present although, since it produces only a small sound, it tends to be little more than a dance decoration. This is the *sogo*, a small double-headed frame drum with an integral wooden handle (H/S 211.322.8). The name is generic. Various alternative names exist: *maegu puk* specifically relates the drum to agriculture, while *pŏpku* indicates a Buddhist connection. There are records of *sogo* made with cloth rather than skin heads, a practice which precludes any effective musical role. Similar drums, however, which typically double as sieves, are not uncommon elsewhere, and there is a parallel with, for example, the Irish *bodhrán*.

Turning to their use at court, the two gongs were described in *Akhak kwebŏm* as the small *sogŭm* and large *taegŭm*, placing emphasis on the material of construction (*kŭm/gŭm* = metal). We are told that they were once played in the first and second wine offerings in the Rite to Royal Ancestors and were allied in Chinese cosmology to autumn, the colour white, and the direction west. The *taegŭm* used a stick wrapped with deerskin, while the *sogŭm* was held in a frame surmounted by a dragon's head.

Court and ritual music provides a home for many percussion instruments originally imported from China. Amongst idiophones, clappers, called *pak* (H/S 111.12), are the instrument of a director. In Korea, *pak* comprise six rectangular hardwood slabs bound with cords through holes cut near their top. The director stands to one side of an ensemble, holding the outer slabs and cracking them together once to begin a piece and three times to finish it. More splendid are sets of clapperless bronze bells (*p'yŏnjong*; H/S 111.242.221) and stone chimes (*p'yŏn'gyŏng*; H/S 111.222), originally part of Huizong's 1116 gift. In China, the equivalent sets date back over 3,000 years and are known as *bianzhong* and *bianqing*, but Koreans claim that the sets now in use in Taiwan were modelled after modern Korean instruments. The Vietnamese *biên khanh* and *biên chung* are related to the Korean versions.

In Korea, each set of *p'yŏnjong* and *p'yŏn'gyŏng* is housed in a magnificent decorated frame with animals and birds carved on the crosspieces and at each foot (Fig. 5.2). The

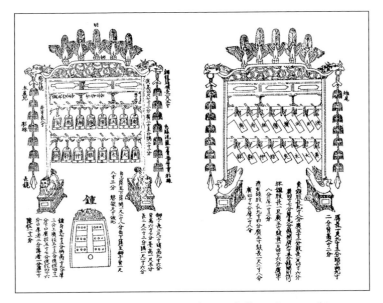

5.2 The *p'yŏnjong* and *p'yŏn'gyŏng* bronze bells and stone chime sets, as depicted in *Akhak kwebŏm*. Bells and chimes are tuned in semitones, ascending in pitch from bottom right to bottom left then top left to top right.

16 elliptical bells are tuned to give a chromatic scale, c–d#´. The 16 L-shaped lithophone chimes sound in parallel an octave higher. Stone for the chimes is carved from calcite quarried since the fifteenth century at Namyang in the central Kyŏnggi province. Both bells and chimes play in the Rite to Confucius, with a single pair—rather than the nine pairs prescribed by the fifteenth-century *Akhak kwebŏm* to be spread along three sides of a square—in each of the terrace ensemble (*tŭngga*) and courtyard ensemble (*hŏn'ga*).

In the rite, they sit adjacent to single clapperless bells (*t'ŭk-chong*; in Chinese, *tezhong*; H/S 111.242.121) and chimes (*t'ŭkkyŏng*; in Chinese, *teqing*; H/S 111.221). Both also play in the two surviving *tangak* pieces, *Nagyangch'un* and *Pohŏja*, where they have replaced a set of 16 iron slabs, the *panghyang* (H/S 111.212). *Panghyang* were used in Korea by 1076, and five sets arrived as part of the first Huizong gift in 1114. They were apparently used in court music until the end of the eighteenth century, since they are depicted as playing at the newly built Kyŏngmo Palace erected by King Chŏngjo (r.1776–1800). Today they play only in the Rite to Royal Ancestors. Contemporary sets have a chromatic range identical to the *p'yŏnjong* but pitched two octaves higher.

Three curious idiophones and four membranophones see use only in the Rite to Confucius. The *ch'uk* (H/S 111.13) is a mortar, a trapeziform wooden box painted green with a thick stick inserted through a central hole. The stick is struck three times against the base to signal the start of a piece. The *ŏ* (H/S 112.212)(Fig. 5.3) is a wooden tiger with a prescribed 27 notches cut on the backbone. A split bamboo stick is dragged down the backbone three times to signal the end of a piece, producing a sound not dissimilar to that of the Caribbean *guiro* scraper. The *pu* (H/S 112.23) is a baked clay vessel. A split stick used on the rim marks the beginning of each melodic note. All four membranophones, drums, have bodies painted royal red. The *chŏlgo* and *chin'go* are barrel drums (H/S 211.222.7), the former hung at an angle and the latter in a vertical plane. In the Rite to Confucius, the *chŏlgo* plays with the terrace ensemble, and the *chin'go*—with skins 110cm in diameter the largest drum still in use—plays with the courtyard ensemble. The *chin'go* is similar to many of the drums that can be found at Buddhist temples. The *nogo* (H/S

5.3 The ŏ played in the Rite to Confucius.

211.222.27) and *nodo* (H/S 232.222.27) are more unusual. They play part of the starting pattern for each piece of music, and the *nogo* also punctuates each fourth note in the regular melody. Each instrument actually consists of two drums mounted at right angles to each other, the *nogo* suspended on a pole inside a decorated wooden frame and the *nodo* pierced by a wooden pole with tigers at its base. The *nodo* (Fig. 5.4) are pellet drums with knotted thongs

5.4 The *nodo* pellet drums.

attached to each side of each body, played by rotating the pole so that the thongs strike the heads.

A number of other percussion instruments are now obsolete or have limited uses. The *ulla* (H/S 111.241.2), China's 'moon cloud' set of 10 plate-gong idiophones, are mounted in a vertical wooden frame. They were used at court banquets during the eighteenth and ninteenth centuries, but only one set, brought from Beijing in 1937, is preserved in Seoul. In South Korea, some composers have recently commissioned brassware (*yugijang*) makers such as Yi Pongju (b.1926), the holder of Asset No. 77, to recreate the *ulla* for experimental music.

A number of barrel drums still exist in this marginal category. The large *chwago*, hung vertically in a simple frame, was first recorded in an eighteenth-century dance depiction. The *kyobanggo*, supported in a horizontal cross-frame so that one head is vertical, was described much earlier in the *Koryŏsa*, but today accompanies only a single dance, *Mugo*, reserved for royalty until this century. The larger *chunggo* was used during the reign of the later King Sŏngjong (r.1469–94; grandson of King Sejo) in sacrifices to the god of war, but only one example survives. The *sakko* and small *ŭnggo* (*sak* = start; *ŭng* = echo) were held vertically in frames decorated with dragons and tigers, but fell into disuse in the nineteenth century. The huge and elaborately decorated 150cm deep *kŏn'go* (*kŏn* = build) had two massive skins and was used at the same events. References to the *kŏn'go* reach back to the Huizong gifts. Four other drums became obsolete overnight when the Japanese forced the Korean court to abandon rites to heavenly and earthly spirits. *Noe* means thunder, and the *noego* and *noedo* were painted black to symbolize their use for heavenly spirits. The *yŏnggo* and *yŏngdo* were painted yellow: *yŏng* means spirit. The *noego* had six and the *yŏnggo* eight conical drums arranged in a ring within a wooden frame. The *noedo* had three and the *yŏngdo* four barrel drums mounted on a pole like the *nodo* and played with similar thongs.

The Korean percussion inventory would be incomplete without mention of the numerous instruments that contribute to the soundscape of streets, mountains, and rural villages. Basic idiophones similar to the clay *pu* were used until recently to accompany singing in the countryside. Examples include gourd and pottery vessels made with the primary function of carrying water, such as the *hŏbŏk* on the southern island of Cheju and the *mul pagaji* in the south-western Chŏlla province. In Chŏlla there were several local variations. In one, the vessel was turned upside down and partially submerged in a bowl of water. A local term, *toshin*, gives an onomatopoeic representation of the resultant sound, and seems to signify a use as an accompanying instrument for prayers. Again, the *mul pagaji* was sometimes transformed into a chordophone (H/S 311.121.21), when a bow designed to tease cotton into strands was vibrated above the resonating vessel. The bow produced the sound *'tungdŏngi'*; this may explain the origin of the title of a common folksong, *Tungdŏngi t'aryŏng*.

Bronze bells, *chong* (H/S 111.242.121), have long been used for civil functions. One, housed within *Poshin'gak*, the belfry at the entrance to Seoul's central street, Chongno, still marks the start of each New Year. Fourteen are preserved as *yuhyŏng munhwajae* (tangible cultural assets); others can be found in virtually every Buddhist temple. Shamans also use bells. In the extreme south-west, single instruments are common; some shamans substitute rice bowl lids with rims. In the south-eastern Kyŏngsang provinces and on Cheju, bowl-shaped gongs are employed for a similar function but are played inverted, with rims resting on a mat or on the floor (H/S 111.241.11). In Seoul and central Korea, *pangul* bell trees (H/S 112.112) were common until recently. These are still used by shamans born in North Korea who migrated to Seoul during the Korean war. Since shamanism is officially no longer practised in North

Korea, no data is available about their use north of the partition.

Buddhist temples in both parts of the peninsula bristle with wind chimes and small brass fish plaques, while monks strike wooden slit drums known as *mokt'ak* to punctuate prayers and as they seek alms. The *mokt'ak* are like temple blocks, and cognates include the Chinese *muyu* and the Japanese *mokugyo*. Cymbals (H/S 111.142) are variously described as *chabara*, *para*, and *chegŭm*. Buddhists preserve a cymbal dance known as *para ch'um*. Cymbals were also used in shamanistic rituals from the northern Hwanghae and P'yŏngan provinces, and still feature in the processional *Taech'wit'a*. A final 'instrument' (an example of which is preserved at the Fitzwilliam Museum in Cambridge, England) will be familiar to anyone who has stayed in South Korean cities. This is the *yŏtchangsu kawi*, large, resonant iron scissors that are used to clip the air to announce and accompany the dawn calls of rubbish collectors.

Readings and Recordings

Readings on Korean Musical Instruments

Howard, Keith, *Korean Musical Instruments: A Practical Guide*, Seoul: Se-kwang Music Publishing, 1988.

Provine, Robert, C., Entries on Korean instruments, in Stanley Sadie (ed.), *The New Grove Dictionary of Musical Instruments*, London: Macmillan, 1984.

Chang Sahun, *Han'guk akki taegwan* (Comprehensive account of Korean musical instruments), Seoul: Han'guk kugak hakhoe, 1969 (in Korean).

Chang Sahun, *Kugak taesajŏn* (Dictionary of Korean music), Seoul: Segwang ŭmak ch'ulp'ansa, 1984 (in Korean).

Kim Kisu, Scorebooks for *tanso*, *taegŭm*, *haegŭm*, and *kayagŭm*, Seoul: Kungnip kugak kodŭng hakkyo/Ŭnha ch'ulp'ansa, 1961–79 (in Korean).

Munye ch'ulp'ansa (assorted authors), *Chosŏn minjok akki ch'ongsŏ* (Series on Korean people's instruments), Vols. 1–10, P'yŏngyang: Munye ch'ulp'ansa, 1983–9 (in Korean).

Pak Chŏngnam, *Paehap kwanhyŏnak p'yŏnsŏngbŏp* (A method for the harmonious combination of orchestral instruments), P'yŏngyang: Munye ch'ulp'ansa, 1990 (in Korean).

Pak Pŏmhun, *Kugakki ihae* (A practical guide: Korean musical instruments), Seoul: Segwang ŭmak ch'ulp'ansa, 1991 (in Korean).

Readings on Korean Music

Hahn Man-young, *Kugak: Studies in Korean Traditional Music* (Trans. Keith Howard and Inok Paek), Seoul:

Tamgudang, 1991.

Howard, Keith, *Bands, Songs, and Shamanistic Rituals: Folk Music in Korean Society*, Seoul: Korea Branch of the Royal Asiatic Society (2d ed.), 1990.

Korean Traditional Performing Arts Centre, *The Traditional Music and Dance of Korea*, Seoul: Korean Traditional Performing Arts Centre, 1994.

Lee Hye-Ku, *Essays on Korean Traditional Music* (Trans. Robert C. Provine), Seoul: Korea Branch of the Royal Asiatic Society, 1981.

Pratt, Keith, *Korean Music: Its History and Its Performance*, Seoul: Jung Eum Sa, and London: Faber Music, 1987.

Provine, Robert, *Essays on Sino-Korean Musicology: Early Sources for Korean Ritual Music*, Seoul: Il Ji Sa, 1988.

Song Bang-Song, *The Sanjo Tradition of Korean Kŏmun'go Music*, Seoul: Jung Eum Sa, 1986.

Song Bang-Song, *Source Readings in Korean Music*, Seoul: Korean National Commission for UNESCO, 1980.

Recordings

Instrumental music is featured on an array of recordings produced or recorded in South Korea, including: *Kugak ŭi hyangyŏn* (Banquet of Korean music)(50 LPs, G169–G218), Seoul: Chungang Ilbosa, 1988; *Korean Traditional Music 1–5* (5 CDs, SKCD-K-0001–5), *Yŏngsan hoesang* (1 CD, SKCD-K-0007), *Sanjo* (5 CDs, SKCD-K-0008/10/11/12/60), and *Chongmyo cheryeak* (Rite to royal ancestors)(1 CD, SKCD-K-0059), all Seoul: SKC, 1987–8; *Han'guk ŭmak sŏnjip* (Selections of Korean classical music)(LP sets, vol. 1, 1972, to vol. 19, 1990, and CDs, vol. 20, 1991 and continuing), Seoul: Korean Traditional Performing Arts Centre; *Han'guk ŭmak sŏnjip* (Selections of Korean classical music)(cassette sets, vols. 1–12, CS054-CS065), Seoul: Seung Eum, 1985–8; *Han'guk ŭi chŏnt'ong ŭmak* (A selection of Korean traditional music)(4 CDs, JCDS-0194–7), Seoul: Jigu,

1991; *Han'guk ŭi chŏnt'ong ŭmak: 21 segirŭl wihan KBS-FM ŭi pangsong ŭmak sirijŭ* (Korean traditional music: Music for the 21st century presented by KBS-FM)(19 CDs, KIFM001–009 and Hae-Dong 110–119), Seoul: Korean Broadcasting System, 1992, 1994; *'93 ilyo myŏngin myŏngch'angjŏn 1–12* (1993 Sunday great musicians' series)(12 CDs, SRCD-1179–96), Seoul: Cantabile, 1993.

A fascinating set of 10-inch discs, produced in the 1960s and distributed to scholars, libraries, and international organizations by the Korean Cultural Treasures Institute (*Han'guk munhwajae yŏn'guhoe*), was *Buddhist Temple Bells of Korea* (*Han'guk ŭi pŏmjong*). A more recent collection, again never issued commercially but distributed in 1990 to Korean consulates and foreign libraries and radio stations by the Korean Overseas Information Service, was *The Sounds of Korea*. This is a comprehensive compilation of 24 CDs coupled with a useful 132-page book in English.

JVC World Sounds has a number of Korean releases (currently, VICG-5018–5023, VICG-5214, and VICG-5261). *Samul Nori* provides the title for a number of albums, including 72093-1 (New York: Nonesuch Explorer, 1984/1991), 32DG64 (Tokyo: CBS-Sony, 1987), KCD-007 (Seoul: Seorabul, 1987), SKCD-K-0236 (Seoul: SKC, 1988), RZF1002 (Tokyo: Rhizome Sketch, 1989), and ORC-1014 (Seoul: Oasis, 1991); Samul Nori also play for one track on *A Week in the Real World, Part 1* (CDRW25, London: Real World/Virgin, 1992) and on *Then Comes the White Tiger* (ECM 1499, Munich: ECM, 1994). Other worthwhile titles include *Korean Court Music* (LL7206, New York: Lyrichord), *Korean Social and Folk Music* (LLST7211, New York: Lyrichord), *Korea: Musique instrumentale de la tradition classique* (C558701, Paris: Ocora), *Korea: Court Music* (PS65023, Paris: Playasound), and *Korea: UNESCO Music and Musicians of the World* (D8010, Paris: Auvidis). This last is a CD re-release of *Korean Music: UNESCO Collection of Musical Sources, Art Music from the Far East, VIII-1* (6586-011, Philips).

Index

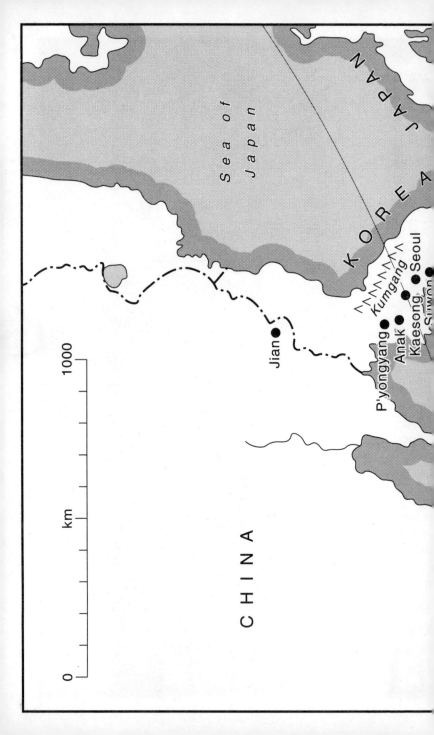